Simply Stews

Also by Susan Wyler

Cooking from a Country Farmhouse
Cooking for a Crowd
Tailgate Parties

Simply Stews

More Than 100 Savory One-Pot Meals

SUSAN WYLER

HarperPerennial
A Division of HarperCollinsPublishers

HarperCollins books may be purchased for educational,
business, or sales promotional use. For information
please write: Special Markets Department, Harper-
Collins Publishers, Inc., 10 East 53rd Street, New York,
NY 10022.

FIRST EDITION

Designed by Stephanie Tevonian

Library of Congress Cataloging-in-Publication Data

Wyler, Susan.
    Simply stews : more than 100 savory one-pot
meals / Susan Wyler. — 1st ed.
        p.   cm.
    Includes index.
    ISBN 0-06-095144-3
    1. Stews.   2. Cookery, International.   I. Title.
TX693.W95   1995
641.8'23—dc20   95-25214

97 98 99 ❖/RRD 10 9 8 7

Contents

Elegant Ragout of Chicken with Artichokes and Asparagus, easy Triple-Mustard Chicken Dijon, Spicy Chicken Creole, succulent Duck with Olives, and homey Chicken Succotash with Corn, Lima Beans, and Buttermilk are a sampling of the variety included in these two dozen tasty ways to stew chicken, turkey, and duck.

Whether you are entertaining friends or feeding your family, you'll find plenty of perfect choices here: Beef Stew with Roasted Garlic, Mushrooms, and Potatoes, Tangy Cabernet Beef with Bacon and Onions, Spicy Party Chili with Scotch Bonnet Peppers and Tequila, Veal Shanks with Wild Mushrooms and Madeira, and Venison Stew with Armagnac and Prunes.

Versatile, lean pork is paired here with compatible vegetables to create colorful, zesty stews such as Green Pork Chili with Kale and Hominy, Barbecued Country Ribs Stew with Sweet Potatoes and Black-Eyed Peas, Lion's Head Casserole, and Adobo of Pork with Chayote, Carrots, and Sugar Snap Peas.

Savory lamb, sweetly spiced or simmered with fragrant herbs, creates deeply flavored stews: Fruited Lamb Curry with Almonds and Mint, Lamb Stew with Spring Vegetables, and Lamb Stew au Ratatouille.

Chicken and Other Poultry Stews

Beef, Veal, and Venison Stews

Pork Stews

Lamb Stews

Fish and Shellfish Stews

Vegetable and Bean Stews

Stocks for Stew

Fish and Shellfish Stews . 161

Quick to cook and exceptionally *appetizing, these seafood stews—such as Shrimp Curry with Mango and Pineapple, Shellfish Fra Diavolo, Thai-Style Crab and Fish Stew with Cilantro and Lime, and Ragout of Swordfish with Shiitake Mushrooms—are fabulous light meals in a bowl.*

Vegetable and Bean Stews . 193

Whether you are a vegetarian, *and are trying to eat a greater proportion of complex carbohydrates and fiber, or just want a tasty meatless dish for variety, you'll find such recipes as Garlicky Beans and Greens, Smoky Vegetable Chili with Pinto Beans, and Curried Vegetables with Chick-Peas and Raisins immensely satisfying.*

Stocks for Stews . 229

A *few simple stocks are all you'll need to produce the best-tasting, most stylish stews around. Here are recipes for stocks to make now and freeze for later.*

Index . 237

Acknowledgments

Many thanks to Anne Marie Noone and Amy Howarth, who helped test the recipes for this book; to Bobbi Fazzi, who kept us all in order; and to my friends, especially Pamela and Paul Kelly, Pat and Larry Roberts, Kevin Huffman and Allan Duncan, Susan Thornton and Gerry Hough, Barbara Remington, and Peggy, Dave, and Jason Soden, who were great eaters. My sincere appreciation to my editor, Susan Friedland, for her keen eye, thoughtful editing, and love of good food.

Introduction

From French fricassees to Italian ragouts, from Chinese hot pots to honest American stews, one-pot dishes hold a special place in the culinary affections of cooks around the world. There is something reassuring about the sturdiness of the stewpot, a vessel both for cooking and serving; there is reassurance also in the reminder that much can come from little. Almost any food that is legitimately ladled into a big bowl, with its mix of ingredients bathed in hot savory sauce, promises satisfaction in the eating. And there is great pleasure in the smells, sight, and taste of a well-made stew. Whether served as the centerpiece of the dinner, or as the entire main course in a single offering, these complexly flavored recipes represent much of the finest home cooking.

Many meat stews are low-maintenance, long-simmering affairs that bubble away on top of the stove — or in the oven — with little or no attention from the cook. For hours they fill the kitchen with their tantalizing aroma, galvanizing aromatic attention, announcing the call to table with promises of intense satisfaction long before the dinner hour chimes. Beautifully browned, caramelized cubes of succulent meat mingle their juices with various aromatics, earthy vegetables, floral herbs, and subtle stocks, often punctuated with the tart fruitiness of a red or white wine and the sprightly acidity of tomato or lemon juice, creating finally a whole dish that is, indeed, much more than the sum of its component ingredients.

Meat stews require time to develop character and flavor. Beef stew is a relaxing affair. Some versions do best after a long stretch, even a day or two of marinating; the slow cooking can extend for a couple of hours, to soften the chunks of meat into meltingly tender morsels, giving pleasure in texture as well as in taste. And pork requires a relatively long (up to one and a half hours) braising to add moisture to the lean meat.

Other kinds of stews, however, are surprisingly quick. Most chicken stews are ready in sixty minutes or less. Because I frequently remove the skin to avoid excess fat, many of these recipes can be finished in a fraction of the usual time. And especially for summer, when you don't want to spend too long in a hot kitchen, I've included chicken stews made with chunks of skinless, boneless white meat that cook in a flash. Most vegetable stews can be on the table in half an hour or less. And seafood stews are timed in minutes.

One other class of stew scattered throughout this collection is what I call "twice-cooked stews": that is, potpies. Almost all savory pies begin with a filling that could be served as a stew in a bowl, but becomes all the more appealing when topped with a flaky pastry, puff pastry, biscuit, or alternative (such as mashed potato) crust and baked just before serving.

Depending upon the vegetables added to the stew, which can lose texture, and with the exception of seafood stews, which, in general, are best eaten as soon as they are ready, almost all stews improve upon reheating. In fact, because of the leaner cuts I have used in many of these recipes, cooling in the tasty liquid and then rewarming makes the meat in many of these stews more succulent. And because so many have complex flavors, often including tomatoes and wine, they do very well with a comfortable rest between the finishing and the eating.

An added boon for the busy cook is that many stews survive at least two or three months in the freezer with no ill effects. In fact, stews that are covered with plenty of liquid will keep extremely well for up to six months. If I feel like making a stew and there are only a few of us to dinner, I'll serve half and freeze the remainder in a self-sealing plastic freezer storage bag or heavy plastic-lidded container for a day when I don't feel like cooking. It's a great luxury then to pull dinner ready-made right out of the freezer. In general, the only stews that do not keep well are seafood stews and those containing root vegetables, such as carrots and potatoes, which I think become too mealy with long storage, and green beans or sugar snap or snow peas, which lose their color and their texture if frozen.

All the recipes in this book were designed to be as tasty as they could be and as colorful as possible. It is important to keep in mind that while stews are sometimes thought of as economical, as with all good food — and much else in life — quality counts. The quality and freshness of all the ingredients added will have a direct effect on the taste of the finished dish. So will the combinations of flavors and textures you choose to put together. While stew implies a blending of tastes, you can't just throw anything together in a pot.

Several of the recipes in this book are variations on the classics: Tangy Cabernet Beef with Bacon and Onions, for example, is my version of boeuf bourguignon; and Chardonnay Chicken with Wild Mushrooms is an updated approach to coq au vin. But while nothing is new under the sun, I have tried to develop a number of stews that are contemporary in their ingredients or pairings of flavors and attentive to the adventurous spirit and love of big taste — from the Southwest, Mexico, and the Mediterranean — that seems to be the happy trend in American dining. Some are stylish in an extravagant way that makes them a natural for your most important dinner parties. They pull out all the stops. Lobster Stewed in Whiskey Cream with Grilled Portobello Mushrooms and Asparagus, for example, is so luxurious and rich, I like to serve it as a first course, before a simple steak or leg of lamb. It is a knockout, guaranteed to garner raves. Other stews are up-to-date in their attention to nutrition. Wherever possible, I've reduced portions of meat and upped the vegetables — for color and flavor as well as for dietary balance.

In many recipes, fat is reduced as much as possible, not only through skimming and straining, but by avoiding it as much as possible in the first place: choosing lean cuts, trimming off all external fat and skin, and using small amounts of olive oil for the initial browning. While traditionally stews have often been made with the cheapest, fattiest cuts, which are often also the most flavorful, I found that in many instances marinating leaner meats and cooking skinned and trimmed chickens and ducks produced wonderful savory stews with less cooking time than those made from their poorer or fattier relations.

Any flavor lost from fat has been more than compensated for through the addition of plenty of herbs, spices, garlic, onions, and intensely piquant ingredients like olives, sun-dried tomatoes, capers, and lemon juice. Where appropriate, sauces are reduced and extra flavor is added with wine, dried fruit, vegetables, and chiles. While the results are more healthful, they are also more economical in that there is less meat per person and more vegetables than in many traditional stews. Portions listed are for main courses, though particularly in the case of the fish and shellfish stews, many would serve well as a first course, in which case they would feed about half again as many people.

Technique is a little difficult to discuss with the range of stews included in this book. In general, meat and chicken stews follow a rather classic form of occasionally marinating, then browning the meat first, adding aromatics and liquid—which might be wine, tomato juice, stock, or even water—herbs, spices, and any other seasonings, and simmering the whole, whether on top of the stove or in the oven, until the meat is meltingly tender and the flavors are mingled together. Most often, I have opted for the top of the stove, because I believe it conserves energy and is easier to turn to for a moment to stir, skim, or taste. Where I feel the oven is a better option for more even all-round slow cooking, I've recommended that instead. In most cases, you are free to switch these around if you prefer—if you need the stovetop free, for example—but do check toward the end, because the cooking times may vary a bit.

I have been somewhat unorthodox in my use of flour as a coating. Traditionally, a light flour coating helps seal in juices and adds a little thickener to the sauce. In most instances, I feel I have more control over the browning of the meat and insurance that the flour will not burn on the bottom of the pot if I first brown the meat and then add the flour in carefully measured amounts either as a roux or a slurry. For a discussion of stocks for stews, see the last chapter on page 229.

Good stew requires good wine. For cooking, I take a middle course: no plonk and no extravagance either. Do the best you can. Just don't let the flavor of the wine overpower the sauce. For a light fish stew, a sauvignon blanc is often a better choice than an oaky Chardonnay. For a red, I like a lighter Cabernet Sauvignon or a dry, medium-bodied Italian. For drinking, I go red wherever possible. Bordeaux or a California Cabernet Sauvignon is an excellent pairing with many of the stronger beef stews. I am partial to the pinot noir grape and find that Burgundy, which is lighter than many people think, goes with a wide range of stews, both meat and chicken. I like the fruitiness of a cru Beaujolais, such as Brouilly and Moulin à Vent, or even Juliénas, with some of the spicier stews. And simple Italian reds, even a bargain-priced Montepulciano d'Abruzzi, will be fine for quaffing with sauces that are heavy on the tomato base or laden with herbs and spices. The grander light stews, lobster or chicken with wild mushrooms, pair well with a slightly aged Chardonnay, a Chablis, or Puligny-Montrachet, if you can do it. For the more acidic light stews, I am happy with a fumé or a sauvignon blanc.

When stew is the star of the meal, menu-planning sometimes stumps the experts. Good bread is almost always welcome to sop up the gravy, and a simple starch — potatoes, rice, or noodles — if not already included, is usually all it needs, since most stews are a meal in a dish. To start with, you certainly don't want to lead off with a soup. Depending upon the number of people coming over and the formality of the occasion, or whether it is a small, simple family supper, you have many good choices. Because stews contain a complex blend of ingredients, the food before and after should be kept simple. Prosciutto with melon or with fresh figs, tomato and mozzarella salad, arugula salad with baked goat cheese, and individual shells of sliced sea scallops topped with garlicky bread crumbs and run under the broiler for a few moments are several of my stew meal standard starters. Alternatively, I might pass hors d'oeuvres before the meal and offer no first course. In that event, I almost always follow the centerpiece stew with a simple salad and an assortment of good cheeses, ending with an intensely flavored dessert, often chocolate, sometimes fruit.

Chicken and Other Poultry Stews

here's no doubt that chicken is the most popular meat in America. The same versatility that makes it so perfect for soups, salads, roasting, sautéing, and grilling makes it ideal for stewing. Whether browned and then braised in liquid as in a classical ragout, or simply poached in a flavorful broth, chicken slips easily from everyday to elegant, from subtle and smooth to hot and spicy, from all-American to international. All it takes is a change of dress: a different herb or vegetable, a red or white wine, a simple stock.

Because I personally dislike soft chicken skin (and no matter how carefully you flour and brown the bird, long braising in liquid softens it again), and it is in this skin that much of the fat in chicken resides, in many of these recipes I have chosen to remove the skin and any excess fat underneath. In my opinion, there is no appreciable loss in flavor; in fact, the meat in direct contact with the stewing liquid and seasonings imbibes even more taste. Another benefit of removing the skin is that it speeds up the time it takes for the chicken to stew to succulent tenderness. The only disadvantage in some cases is a slightly bare appearance to the pieces of cut-up chicken, which can be

covered easily with brightly colored vegetables and a slightly thickened sauce to nap the meat.

While I was delighted at the loss of cholesterol and calories, one European friend of mine felt that duck was not duck without its unctuous layer of fat. If you feel this way, simply leave the skin on and add on extra time for more complete browning and longer stewing.

Since stews are delightful menu centerpieces in summer as well as in the cooler months, I have designed a number of these recipes using cut-up skinless, boneless chicken breasts, stews that cook in fifteen minutes or less. Spicy Chicken Creole and Summer Chicken Ragout with Sweet Corn, Fresh Tomatoes, and Cilantro are two of these quick and delicious dishes. And because they are in chunks, they work well as easy-to-serve buffet stews, to be ladled over rice or pasta for easy entertaining.

Bouillabaisse of Chicken

6 Servings   **H**ere is a bright-tasting stew, aromatic with leeks, orange zest, and Pernod and enriched with a homemade spicy mayonnaise laced with a heady dose of garlic. Serve with crusty sourdough bread and a tossed salad.

1 chicken (about 3 pounds)
1 whole chicken breast, split in half
2 tablespoons Pernod
3 tablespoons extra-virgin olive oil
2 teaspoons grated orange zest
2 garlic cloves, crushed through a press
1 teaspoon salt
1 teaspoon fennel seeds, crushed
¾ teaspoon dried thyme leaves
½ teaspoon freshly ground black pepper
½ teaspoon hot paprika
4 medium leeks (white and lighter green parts), split lengthwise, rinsed well, and cut into 1-inch lengths
3 large plum tomatoes, peeled, seeded, and coarsely chopped, or 1½ cups drained chopped canned tomatoes
2 pinches of saffron threads (about ⅜ teaspoon)
1 cup dry white wine
3 cups Rich Chicken Stock (page 232)
Spicy Garlic Mayonnaise (recipe follows)

1. Cut the chicken into 8 pieces: 2 drumsticks, 2 thighs, 2 wings, and the 2 breast halves. Cut all the chicken breasts crosswise in half. There will be 14 pieces in all. Remove as much chicken skin and fat as possible.

2. In a small bowl, blend together the Pernod, 1 tablespoon of the olive oil, the orange zest, garlic, salt, fennel, thyme, black pepper, and hot paprika to make a paste. Place the chicken in a shallow dish and rub the spice paste all over the chicken. Set aside at room temperature.

3. In a large flameproof casserole, heat the remaining 2 tablespoons olive oil over moderate heat. Add the leeks and cook, stirring occasionally, until softened but not browned, 3 to 5 minutes. Add the tomatoes and crumble the saffron into the pot. Cook, stirring, 2 minutes. Pour in the wine, bring to boil, and boil 3 minutes, or until reduced by about half.

4. Add the chicken stock to the casserole. Add the chicken pieces, scraping any marinade that remains in the bowl into the pot. Bring to a simmer, partially cover, and cook over moderately low heat until the chicken is juicy and tender, about 25 minutes. Serve in soup plates and pass the Spicy Garlic Mayonnaise on the side.

➤ This stew keeps in the refrigerator for up to 3 days. Stored in a tightly covered container, it will freeze well for up to 6 months. The mayonnaise should, however, be freshly prepared.

Spicy Garlic Mayonnaise

Makes about 1½ cups

*C*alled rouille *in French, this hot garlicky sauce adds zest to any kind of bouillabaisse, whether chicken or fish. This is a simple food processor version of the classic, which is traditionally made with a mortar and pestle.*

2 slices of stale French bread, cut ½ inch thick, crusts removed

1 tablespoon Champagne vinegar or white wine vinegar

1 whole egg

1 egg yolk

5 garlic cloves, crushed through a press

1 tablespoon tomato paste

1 tablespoon fresh lemon juice

½ teaspoon cayenne

½ teaspoon salt

½ cup light olive oil

⅓ cup extra-virgin olive oil

1. Soak the bread in a small bowl with the vinegar and 1 tablespoon water. Squeeze dry and place in a food processor.

2. Add the whole egg, egg yolk, crushed garlic, tomato paste, lemon juice, cayenne, and salt. Puree until smooth.

3. With the machine on, slowly add the olive oil and extra-virgin olive oil in a thin stream through the feed tube. Scrape into a bowl. Cover and refrigerate until serving time.

Brunswick Stew

This is a kitchen garden recipe, perfect for the corn, lima bean, and tomato harvest. While lore has it the dish was originally developed for squirrel, it is a natural for chicken and also works well with rabbit. You can omit the ham if you prefer, but the smokiness enhances the flavor.

1 (3½ to 4-pound) chicken

⅓ cup flour

1 teaspoon salt

½ teaspoon freshly ground black pepper

½ teaspoon dried thyme leaves

⅛ teaspoon cayenne

3 tablespoons vegetable oil

2 medium onions, chopped

6 ounces Black Forest or other lean smoked ham, cut into ½-inch
    dice (about 1 cup)

4 cups Rich Chicken Stock (page 232) or reduced-sodium
    canned broth

1 (28-ounce) can peeled whole tomatoes, quartered and
    well drained

1 small green bell pepper, cut into ½-inch dice

1 bay leaf

2 cups fresh shelled lima beans or 1 (10-ounce) package frozen
    baby lima beans, thawed

2 cups corn kernels, from 3 or 4 ears of fresh corn, or use canned
    or frozen

1. Cut the chicken into 10 serving pieces: 2 drumsticks, 2 thighs, 2 wings, and 4 pieces of breast (cut both sides crosswise in half). Trim off as much fat as possible. Rinse and let drain but do not pat dry.

2. In a shallow bowl, mix the flour with the salt, pepper, thyme, and cayenne. Dredge the damp chicken pieces in the seasoned flour. In a large skillet, heat 2 tablespoons of the oil over moderately high heat. Dredge the chicken again

if the coating looks damp and shake any excess back into the bowl; reserve the excess seasoned flour to use for thickening later. Add the chicken pieces to the pan in a single layer without crowding, in batches if necessary, and cook, turning, until golden brown, about 7 minutes per batch. Lower the heat if necessary about halfway through, so the fat doesn't burn. Remove the chicken to a large flame-proof casserole.

3. Add the remaining 1 tablespoon oil and the onions to the skillet. Cook over moderate heat, stirring occasionally, until soft, about 3 minutes. Add the ham and cook until lightly browned, about 3 minutes longer. Sprinkle the reserved seasoned flour over the ham and onions and cook, stirring, 30 to 45 seconds. Pour in half the stock. Bring to a boil, scraping up any brown bits from the bottom of the pan with a wooden spoon. Boil, stirring, until slightly thickened. Pour everything in the skillet over the chicken in the casserole.

4. Add the tomatoes, the remaining stock, the green pepper, and the bay leaf. Bring to a boil, reduce the heat to moderately low, and simmer, partially covered, 15 minutes.

5. Add the lima beans and corn and simmer uncovered until the chicken and vegetables are tender, 10 to 12 minutes longer. Skim any fat off the top of the sauce. Remove and discard the bay leaf and season with additional salt and pepper to taste before serving.

➤ Stored in a tightly covered container, this stew will keep well in the refrigerator for up to 3 days or in the freezer for up to 3 months.

Chardonnay Chicken with Wild Mushrooms

4 to 6 Servings

Because they are added only as a flavor reinforcement, you can use the little bits of porcini left at the bottom of the package for this recipe. Since mushrooms, especially portobellos, tend to darken and continue to loose their juices upon standing, this recipe is best served within several hours of making it.

1 (3½- to 4-pound) chicken
Salt
Freshly ground pepper
2 tablespoons dried porcini mushrooms
¼ cup olive oil
2 cups Chardonnay or other dry white wine
2 cups Rich Chicken Stock (page 232) or reduced-sodium
    canned broth
1 teaspoon dried tarragon
4 tablespoons unsalted butter
½ pound shiitake mushrooms, stemmed, caps halved
    or quartered
3 medium shallots, chopped (¼ cup)
½ pound Italian brown (cremini) mushrooms or medium fresh
    white mushrooms, quartered
½ pound portobello mushrooms, halved and thickly sliced
1½ teaspoons fresh lemon juice
Dash of cayenne
2 teaspoons cornstarch
½ cup heavy cream
2 tablespoons chopped parsley

1. Rinse the chicken and pat dry. Cut into 10 serving pieces: 2 drumsticks, 2 thighs, 2 wings, and 4 pieces of breast (cut both sides crosswise in half). Season with salt and pepper.

2. In a small heatproof bowl, soak the porcini in 1 cup boiling water until soft, about 20 minutes.

3. Meanwhile, in a large flameproof casserole, heat 2 tablespoons of the oil over moderately high heat. Add the chicken in 2 batches and sauté, turning, until golden brown, about 7 minutes per batch. Remove the chicken to a plate and pour off all the oil from the pan.

4. Add the wine to the casserole and bring to a boil, scraping up any brown bits from the bottom of the pan. Return the chicken to the pan and add the chicken stock, ½ teaspoon of the tarragon, ½ teaspoon salt, and ¼ teaspoon pepper. Bring to a bare simmer, cover the pan, and cook over moderately low heat for 20 to 25 minutes, or until the chicken is tender.

5. Meanwhile, remove the porcini from their soaking liquid and squeeze them over the bowl to catch any extra juices. Rinse the porcini to remove any sand or grit; then chop them. Strain and reserve the soaking liquid.

6. In a large skillet, melt 2 tablespoons of the butter in 1 tablespoon of the oil. Add half the shiitake mushrooms and sauté over moderately high heat for 2 minutes. Add half the shallots, half the Italian brown mushrooms, and half the portobellos and cook, tossing frequently, until lightly browned, 2 to 3 minutes. Scrape the mushrooms into a bowl. Sauté the remaining fresh mushrooms and shallots in the remaining butter and oil. Return all the mushrooms to the pan. Season with the remaining ½ teaspoon tarragon, ¼ teaspoon salt, ⅛ teaspoon freshly ground pepper, the lemon juice, and the cayenne. Add the chopped porcini and reserved soaking liquid to the skillet and boil, stirring, until the liquid is reduced by half, 1 to 2 minutes. Scrape the mushrooms and liquid into the casserole and simmer for 10 minutes.

7. Blend the cornstarch with the cream until smooth. Stir into the stew and simmer for 2 minutes. Garnish with the parsley and serve.

➤ As noted above, this stew darkens within hours of being made. However, if you don't mind the change in color (from light beige to a muddy brown), it does reheat well and, stored in a tightly closed container, will hold its flavor in the freezer for up to 6 months.

Cider-Stewed Chicken with Fall Vegetables

4 Servings

S*weet spices and fresh cider lend a delightful woodsy note to this one-dish meal in a bowl. Serve with good whole-grain bread and a tossed salad.*

1 (3- to 3½-pound) chicken

¼ cup flour

Salt

Freshly ground pepper

2 tablespoons butter

1 tablespoon vegetable oil

2 large shallots, minced

2 cups fresh cider

1 cup dry white wine

½ teaspoon dried thyme leaves

2 whole cloves

1 cinnamon stick

1 small bay leaf

1 cup Rich Chicken Stock (page 232) or reduced-sodium
    canned broth

1 teaspoon cider vinegar

2 medium carrots, peeled, halved lengthwise, cut diagonally into
    1-inch pieces

2 medium red potatoes (organic if possible), scrubbed and
    cut into 1-inch wedges

¼ pound sugar snap peas

¼ cup heavy cream

1. Cut the chicken into 10 pieces: 2 drumsticks, 2 thighs, 2 wings, and 4 pieces of breast (cut both sides crosswise in half). Trim off as much fat as possible. Season the flour with salt and pepper. Dredge the chicken in the flour and shake any excess back into the bowl.

2. In a large flameproof casserole, melt the butter in the oil over moderate to moderately high heat. Add the chicken in 2 batches and sauté, turning, until golden, 5 to 7 minutes per batch. Remove to a plate. Pour off all but 1 tablespoon oil from the pan.

3. Add the shallots to the same casserole and cook over moderate heat until softened and fragrant, about 1 minute. Pour in the cider and wine and bring to a boil, scraping up all the browned bits from the bottom of the pan. Tie the thyme, cloves, cinnamon, and bay leaf in a cheesecloth bag and add to the liquid. Boil for 5 minutes.

4. Add the chicken stock, vinegar, ½ teaspoon salt, and ¼ teaspoon freshly ground pepper. Return the chicken to the pan along with any juices that have collected on the plate. Add the carrots and potatoes. Cover and simmer over low heat until the chicken are vegetables are tender, 25 to 30 minutes.

5. Meanwhile, bring a medium saucepan of water to a boil. Add the sugar snap peas and boil until just tender, about 2 minutes. Drain and rinse under cold running water; drain well.

6. When the chicken is done, remove it to a serving dish; cover to keep warm. Skim as much fat as possible from the top of the liquid in the casserole. Dissolve 1½ tablespoons of the reserved seasoned flour in 2½ tablespoons additional stock or water. Stir into the sauce. Boil over high heat 1 to 2 minutes, until slightly thickened. Stir in the cream and season the sauce with additional salt and pepper to taste. Return the chicken to the stew. Add the sugar snap peas and simmer a minute or two to heat through.

➤ Stored in a tightly closed container, this stew will freeze well for up to 3 months, but the sugar snap peas will lose their texture.

Coq au Vin

6 to 8 Servings

It was impossible to write a book of stews without including a recipe for coq au vin, *or "chicken in wine," the great French classic. This is my version — heavy on the bacon and onions, full of mushrooms, and with an intense, dark sauce.*

½ pound thick-sliced lean bacon

2 chickens (3 to 3½ pounds each)

Salt

Freshly ground pepper

3½ tablespoons olive oil

1 medium onion, finely chopped

3 plum tomatoes, peeled, seeded, and chopped

⅓ cup cognac

2 cups Brown Chicken Stock (page 233)

4 cups dry red wine

2 garlic cloves, crushed through a press

1½ teaspoons fresh lemon thyme leaves or ¾ teaspoon dried thyme

1 bay leaf

6 tablespoons butter

2 packages (10 ounces each) fresh tiny pearl onions, preferably
*   1 red and 1 white, peeled (see* Note*)*

1 pound fresh mushrooms, preferably brown Italian, quartered

¼ cup flour

2 tablespoons chopped parsley

1. Cut the bacon crosswise into ¼-inch-wide strips. Bring a medium saucepan of water to a boil. Add the bacon and cook 2 minutes. Drain into a colander and rinse under warm water. Drain well, then pat dry; set aside.

2. Cut the chickens into 10 pieces each: 2 drumsticks, 2 thighs, 2 wings, and 4 pieces of breast (cut both sides crosswise in half). Trim off as much fat as possible; remove the skin if desired. Season the chicken with salt and pepper. In a large flameproof casserole, heat 2 tablespoons of the oil over moderately high heat. Add the chicken in a single layer without crowding, in several batches, and

cook, turning, until lightly browned, 5 to 7 minutes per batch. Reduce the heat if the oil becomes too hot. As the chicken pieces brown, remove them to a platter.

3. Add the chopped onion to the fat in the pan. Cook over moderate heat, stirring occasionally, until it is soft but not brown, about 3 minutes. Add the tomatoes and cook until they thicken to a paste, 3 to 5 minutes. Pour in the cognac and boil 1 minute. Add the stock and bring to a boil, stirring up any brown bits from the bottom of the pan.

4. Return the chicken to the pan, along with any juices that have collected on the platter. Add the bacon, wine, garlic, thyme, bay leaf, 1 teaspoon salt, and ½ teaspoon pepper. Cover and simmer over low heat 25 to 30 minutes, or until the chicken is tender.

5. Meanwhile, in a large skillet, melt 2 tablespoons of the butter in the remaining 1½ tablespoons oil. Add the pearl onions and sauté over moderately high heat, shaking the pan and turning the onions, until they are nicely browned, about 10 minutes. With a slotted spoon, transfer the onions to stew to finish cooking.

6. Add the mushrooms to the fat remaining in the skillet and sauté over moderately high heat until lightly browned, about 5 minutes. Season with salt and pepper to taste and set aside.

7. Remove the chicken and onions to a side dish and cover to keep warm. (If for any reason the onions still feel hard, leave them in the pot.) Skim as much fat as possible off the liquid in the pan. Boil until the liquid is reduced to about 4 cups, about 3 minutes. Remove and discard the bay leaf. In a small bowl, blend the remaining 4 tablespoons butter with the flour to make a paste. Gradually stir into the liquid and boil until thickened, about 2 minutes.

8. Return the chicken and onions to the sauce. Add the mushrooms with their juices and simmer 2 minutes longer. Season with salt and pepper to taste. Serve, garnished with the parsley.

◇ **Note:** To peel small onions, drop into a saucepan of boiling water for about 10 to 15 seconds. Drain into a colander and rinse briefly under cold running water. Cut off the root end and tip; the outer skin should slip off easily.

➤ Stored in a tightly covered container, this stew will freeze exceptionally well for up to 6 months.

Chicken Couscous

8 to 10 Servings

E*ntertaining couldn't be easier than with this pretty, savory one-dish meal, chock full of vegetables and grain. There is plenty of broth, so be sure to provide bowls, and pass extra harissa or other hot sauce on the side.*

3 tablespoons olive oil

3 medium onions, coarsely chopped

5 garlic cloves, chopped

1 tablespoon minced fresh ginger

2 teaspoons ground coriander

1½ teaspoons ground cinnamon

½ teaspoon ground caraway (optional but desirable)

½ teaspoon freshly grated nutmeg

¼ teaspoon saffron threads, crumbled

4 pounds chicken breasts on the bone, skinned and cut in half

1 (28-ounce) can Italian peeled tomatoes, coarsely chopped, juices reserved

2 cups Rich Chicken Stock (page 232) or reduced-sodium canned broth

1 tablespoon dark brown sugar

2 teaspoons salt

½ teaspoon freshly ground pepper

4 carrots, peeled and roll-cut into 1- to 1½-inch pieces (see page 78)

12 small white boiling onions, peeled (see Note, page 15)

½ cup currants or raisins

6 small turnips, peeled and quartered

3 medium boiling potatoes, peeled and quartered

4 small zucchini, cut into 1-inch pieces

⅓ cup toasted sliced almonds

1½ tablespoons fresh lemon juice

1⅓ cups couscous

2 tablespoons harissa, or more to taste

1. In a large pot, heat the olive oil over moderately high heat. Add the chopped onions and cook, stirring occasionally, until golden, about 5 minutes. Add the garlic, ginger, coriander, cinnamon, caraway, nutmeg, and saffron. Cook, stirring, 1 minute.

2. Add the chicken and cook, turning to coat with the spices, until the meat loses most of its pink outside, about 3 minutes. Add the tomatoes with their liquid, the chicken stock, brown sugar, 1 teaspoon of the salt, the pepper, carrots, boiling onions, currants, and 2 cups of water. Bring to a boil, reduce the heat to moderately low, and simmer, partially covered, 10 minutes.

3. Add the turnips and potatoes and simmer 20 minutes longer. Add the zucchini and toasted almonds. Simmer until zucchini is just tender, 7 to 10 minutes. Stir in the lemon juice and season with additional salt and pepper to taste.

4. In a medium saucepan, bring 2 cups of water to a boil with the remaining 1 teaspoon salt. Stir in the couscous, cover, and remove from the heat. Let stand 5 minutes, then fluff with a fork.

5. To serve, divide the couscous among individual bowls. Top with chicken, an assortment of vegetables, and some of the broth from the pot. Ladle 1½ cups of the broth into a small bowl and stir in the harissa. Pass this spicy harissa broth on the side.

➤ While this stew reheats beautifully — in fact, I think it tastes even better the next day or after standing for a few hours — I don't freeze it, because root vegetables, such as carrots, potatoes, and turnips can turn mealy.

Spicy Chicken Creole

4 to 6 Servings

*S*cotch bonnet peppers, those little pumpkin-shaped pale green and yellow peppers that are more and more frequently seen in supermarket produce departments right next to the other chiles, are fiery hot; one is plenty to spice up any dish. They also contribute a unique earthy flavor. If they are not available, substitute two or three jalapeño or serrano peppers or ½ to 1 teaspoon Tabasco sauce. This is a great one-pot party stew. All it needs is a bed of white rice.

- ½ pound well-flavored ham, such as Black Forest or honey-baked, cut into ½-inch cubes
- 3 tablespoons vegetable oil
- 1 red bell pepper, cut into 1- to 1½-inch squares
- 1 green bell pepper, cut into 1- to 1½-inch squares
- 1 large white onion, cut into 1-inch squares
- 1 Scotch bonnet or 2 or 3 fresh chile peppers, seeded and minced
- 3 garlic cloves, chopped
- 1 cup dry white wine
- 1 (28-ounce) can Italian peeled tomatoes, coarsely cut up, juices reserved
- 1 cup reduced-sodium canned chicken broth
- 1 teaspoon dried oregano
- ½ teaspoon dried thyme leaves
- 1 bay leaf
- 1½ tablespoons Worcestershire sauce
- ½ teaspoon salt
- ¼ teaspoon freshly ground pepper
- 1½ to 1¾ pounds skinless, boneless chicken breasts, cut into 1- to 1½-inch pieces

1. In a large flameproof casserole, cook the ham in the oil over moderate heat, stirring occasionally, until lightly browned around the edges, 3 to 5 minutes. With a slotted spoon, remove the ham to a plate. Add the bell peppers to the casserole, raise the heat to moderately high, and cook, stirring often, until the

peppers are softened but still brightly colored, 5 to 7 minutes. Remove to the plate with the ham.

2. Add the onion to the pan, reduce the heat to moderate, and cook, stirring occasionally, until it is softened and just beginning to brown around the edges, about 5 minutes. Add the Scotch bonnet pepper and the garlic and cook 1 minute longer.

3. Pour the wine into the casserole and bring to a boil, scraping up any browned bits from the bottom of the pan. Boil until the liquid is reduced by half, about 2 minutes. Add the tomatoes with their juices, the broth, oregano, thyme, bay leaf, Worcestershire, salt, and pepper. Bring to a boil, reduce the heat, and simmer, partially covered, 20 minutes.

4. Return the ham and peppers to the casserole along with any juices that have collected on the plate. Add the chicken and simmer, uncovered, stirring once or twice, until the chicken is white throughout but still juicy, 7 to 9 minutes. Season with additional salt to taste.

➤ This stew freezes exceptionally well, though whether it is my imagination or not, I think it loses a little heat; so you may want to add a shake or two of hot sauce and a squeeze of fresh lemon juice to brighten up the sauce again after reheating.

Chicken Fricassee with Sugar Snap Peas and Pearl Onions

6 Servings

A fricassee is an old-fashioned type of stew, creamy and smooth, comforting and soul-satisfying. This one is updated with sugar snap peas and pearl onions. Serve with mashed or boiled potatoes, with biscuits, or with noodles.

4 cups Rich Chicken Stock (page 232)
2 whole cloves
1 medium onion, halved
1 celery rib with leaves, coarsely chopped
1 carrot, peeled and coarsely chopped
½ turnip, peeled and coarsely chopped
3 large sprigs of parsley with stems
1 bay leaf
1 chicken (about 3½ pounds)
1 whole chicken breast on the bone
⅓ cup flour
1 teaspoon salt
½ teaspoon freshly ground pepper
5 tablespoons butter
1¼ pounds large pearl or small white boiling onions, peeled
(see Note, page 15)
1 teaspoon dried thyme leaves
½ pound sugar snap peas
⅓ cup heavy cream

1. Put the stock in a large saucepan. Stick the cloves into the onion halves and add to the pan. Add the celery, carrot, turnip, parsley, and bay leaf. Bring to a boil, reduce the heat slightly, and cook, uncovered, for 20 minutes. Strain the stock through a sieve. There should be 3 cups. If there is more, boil to reduce; if there is less, add enough cold water to equal 3 cups.

2. Meanwhile, cut the whole chicken into 10 serving pieces: 2 drumsticks, 2 thighs, 2 wings, and 4 pieces of breast (cut both sides crosswise in half). Trim off as much fat as possible from the chicken and, if desired, remove the skin. In a shallow bowl, mix the flour with the salt and pepper. Dredge the chicken in the seasoned flour to coat. Reserve any excess seasoned flour in the bowl.

3. In a large flameproof casserole, melt 3 tablespoons of the butter. Add the chicken in a single layer without crowding, in batches if necessary, and cook, turning, until lightly browned, about 5 minutes. As the chicken browns, remove to a plate.

4. Add the remaining 2 tablespoons of butter to the casserole and let melt. Sprinkle on 3 tablespoons of the reserved seasoned flour and cook, stirring, 1 minute. Whisk in the 3 cups of stock and bring to a boil, whisking until thickened and smooth.

5. Reduce the heat to a simmer. Add the chicken, pearl onions, and thyme. Simmer about 35 minutes, or until the chicken and onions are tender and cooked through. Meanwhile, in a large saucepan of boiling water, cook the sugar snap peas until they are bright green and just tender, 1½ to 2 minutes. Drain and rinse under cold running water; drain well.

6. With a slotted spoon or skimmer, remove the chicken and onions to a bowl. Skim any fat off the top of the sauce. Add the cream and boil for 2 minutes to reduce slightly. Season with additional salt and pepper to taste. Return the chicken and onions to the sauce. A minute or two before serving, add the sugar snap peas to the fricassee.

➤ While you can reheat this stew or freeze it for up to 3 months, the sugar snap peas will lose their texture.

Indonesian Chicken in Coconut Milk with Lemongrass and Vegetables

4 to 6 Servings

This is a light, quick-cooking chicken stew, with the richness of coconut milk and the pleasing tartness of lemongrass. Serve with steamed white rice.

> 1¼ pounds skinless, boneless chicken breasts
>
> ½ teaspoon salt
>
> ⅛ teaspoon freshly ground pepper
>
> 1½ tablespoons vegetable oil
>
> 3 shallots, sliced
>
> 2 garlic cloves, finely chopped
>
> 1 tablespoon minced fresh ginger
>
> 1½ teaspoons ground coriander
>
> 1 teaspoon ground cumin
>
> ¼ teaspoon turmeric
>
> ⅛ teaspoon cayenne
>
> 1 cup Rich Chicken Stock (page 232) or reduced-sodium
>   canned broth
>
> 1 (14-ounce) can unsweetened coconut milk
>
> ¼ pound green beans, trimmed and cut into 1½-inch lengths
>
> 1 stalk of fresh lemongrass, thinly sliced, 1 tablespoon dried
>   sliced lemongrass tied in a cheesecloth bag, or 1 large strip of
>   lemon zest about 1½ by 3 inches
>
> 2 salam leaves (see Note)
>
> 2 medium carrots, peeled and cut into 1½ by ⅜-inch sticks

1. Trim any fat or gristle from the chicken breasts and cut the meat into thin strips, about 2 by ⅜-inch. Toss with the salt and pepper.

2. In a large skillet, heat the oil. Add the shallots, garlic, and ginger and cook over moderate heat, stirring occasionally, until softened and fragrant, about 2 minutes. Add the coriander, cumin, turmeric, and cayenne and cook 1 minute

longer. Add the chicken and toss to coat with the spices. Cook, stirring often, 2 to 3 minutes to brown lightly.

3. Add the chicken stock, coconut milk, green beans, lemongrass, and salam leaves. Cover and simmer for 10 minutes. Add the carrots and simmer, stirring occasionally, for 10 to 15 minutes, until the vegetables are tender and the sauce is slightly reduced. Remove and discard the salam leaves before serving.

◇ **Note:** Salam leaves are Indonesian bay leaves. They are available in Indian and Asian markets. There is no substitute.

➤ This stew is best freshly made. It can be reheated the next day and can even be frozen for up to 2 months, but the texture of the carrots and green beans will not be as good, and coconut milk has a tendency to separate.

Italian Chicken Stew with Mushrooms and Peppers

4 to 6 Servings C*hicken cacciatore is the common name for this dish. While some versions are not at all subtle, you may not recognize the lightness of the dish when it is made with fresh tomatoes and crisp green peppers as it is here, producing a delightful and easy yet sophisticated stew. I serve it with polenta, but pasta is a fine accompaniment too.*

1 (3½-pound) chicken
Salt
Freshly ground pepper
3 tablespoons olive oil
1 medium onion, sliced
½ pound mushrooms, sliced
3 garlic cloves, sliced
1 cup dry white wine
2 tablespoons dry Marsala
1 pound ripe tomatoes, peeled, seeded, and coarsely chopped
    or 1 (14½-ounce) can recipe-ready diced tomatoes, with
    their juice
1½ teaspoons tomato paste
1 tablespoon chopped fresh oregano or 1 teaspoon dried
Dash of crushed hot red pepper
1 medium green bell pepper, cut into ¼-inch-wide strips
1 teaspoon balsamic vinegar

1. Cut the chicken into 10 pieces: 2 drumsticks, 2 thighs, 2 wings, and 4 pieces of breast (cut both sides crosswise in half). Rinse the chicken and pat dry. Season with the salt and pepper. In a large flameproof casserole, heat the oil over moderately high heat. Add the chicken (in batches if necessary) and cook, turning, until browned, about 7 minutes. Remove to a plate.

2. Add the onion to the pan and cook, stirring occasionally, 3 minutes. Add the mushrooms and garlic and cook, stirring, until the mushrooms are softened, about 3 minutes longer.

3. Pour in the wine and Marsala and bring to a boil, scraping up any browned bits from the bottom of the pan. Add the tomatoes, tomato paste, oregano, ¾ teaspoon salt, and the hot pepper. Bring to a boil again and return the chicken to the casserole, along with any juices that have collected on the plate.

4. Reduce the heat to low, cover, and cook 20 minutes. Skim off as much fat as possible from the top of the sauce. Add the bell pepper and balsamic vinegar and simmer, partially covered, until the chicken is very tender and practically falling off the bone and the sauce has reduced and thickened slightly, about 10 minutes longer. Season with additional salt and pepper to taste.

➤ Stored in a tightly covered container, this stew reheats well and can be frozen for up to 3 months.

Chicken Paprikash
with Peppery Spaetzle

4 to 6 Servings

T*raditionally, the chicken for this dish is turned in the onions and paprika until the skin is lightly colored. Since after stewing this leaves a soft skin, which these days is not palatable to most people, I prefer to remove the skin altogether and get rid of the extra fat.*

> 1 (3½- to 4-pound) chicken
> ½ teaspoon salt
> ½ teaspoon pepper
> 2 tablespoons unsalted butter
> 1½ tablespoons vegetable oil
> 2 medium onions, chopped
> 2½ tablespoons imported sweet paprika
> 2 cups Rich Chicken Stock (page 232) or reduced-sodium
>   canned broth
> Peppery Spaetzle (recipe follows)
> ¾ to 1 cup sour cream, to taste

1. Cut the chicken into 10 pieces: 2 drumsticks, 2 thighs, 2 wings, and 4 pieces of breast (cut both sides crosswise in half). Rinse and pat dry. Remove as much skin and trim off as much excess fat as you can. Season with the salt and pepper.

2. In a large flameproof casserole, melt the butter in the oil over moderately low heat. Add the onions, cover, and cook 2 minutes. Uncover and continue to cook, stirring often, until the onions are golden and just beginning to brown, 8 to 10 minutes longer.

3. Stir the paprika into the onions. Add the chicken to the casserole and cook, turning, until the pieces are coated with the paprika oil and are whitish on the outside, 2 to 3 minutes. Add the stock, stirring up any browned bits from the bottom of the pan. Cover and simmer over low heat 1¼ to 1½ hours, or until the chicken is very tender.

4. Meanwhile, make the spaetzle. When the chicken is done, remove it to a serving dish and cover to keep warm. Stir the sour cream into the sauce; season with additional salt and pepper to taste. Gently fold in the spaetzle, pour over the chicken, and serve.

◇ **Variation:** Turkey Paprikash. Substitute 2 pounds turkey thigh meat, cut into 2-inch chunks, for the chicken. The simmering time will be reduced to 45 to 60 minutes.

➤ Both these stews reheat nicely. Stored in a tightly covered container, either will freeze well for up to 3 months.

Peppery Spaetzle

4 to 6 Servings

2 cups flour

1½ teaspoons salt

¾ teaspoon freshly ground pepper

⅛ teaspoon cayenne

3 whole eggs

1 egg yolk

½ cup plus 2 tablespoons cold water

1. In a medium bowl, whisk together the flour, salt, pepper, and cayenne until well mixed. Make a well in the center. Add the whole eggs and egg yolk to the well and beat lightly with a fork. Blend the water into the eggs and then mix in the flour, gradually incorporating it from the sides of the well. The batter should be thick enough to offer resistance when you pick some up on a spoon, but it should drop off the spoon easily. If the batter is too thick, mix in a little more water, 1 tablespoon at a time. If it is too thin, add more flour, 1 tablespoon at a time.

2. Bring a large wide saucepan of salted water to a boil. If you happen to have a spaetzle cutter, use it. If not, using 2 teaspoons, quickly scoop out rounded half-teaspoons of the batter with 1 spoon and scrape off into the boiling water with the other; the dumplings with flatten out into little flying saucers when they hit the water. Cook 10 minutes. Drain gently into a colander.

Indian Three-Onion Chicken Curry

4 to 6 Servings

*C*hicken do-pyaz, *or chicken with lots and lots of onions, has always been one of my favorite Indian curries. Serve with basmati rice and lemony green beans or cauliflower.*

> *3 pounds chicken thighs*
> *Salt*
> *Freshly ground pepper*
> *3 medium onions*
> *3 garlic cloves, chopped*
> *2 tablespoons chopped fresh ginger*
> *1 tablespoon ground coriander*
> *2 teaspoons paprika*
> *1½ teaspoons ground cumin*
> *¼ to ½ teaspoon cayenne, to taste*
> *¼ teaspoon turmeric*
> *2 tablespoons vegetable oil*
> *3 shallots, thinly sliced*
> *2 cups Rich Chicken Stock (page 232) or reduced-sodium*
> *canned broth*

1. Remove the skin and fat from the chicken. Season with salt and pepper. In a food processor, grind together 1½ onions, garlic, ginger, coriander, paprika, cumin, cayenne, and turmeric. Thinly slice the remaining onions.

2. In a large flameproof casserole, heat the vegetable oil. Add the sliced onions and shallots and cook over moderate heat until they turn golden and begin to brown, 7 to 10 minutes. Add the onion spice paste and cook, stirring, 2 minutes. Add the chicken and cook, turning, until no longer pink, about 5 minutes.

3. Add the chicken stock and ½ teaspoon salt, reduce the heat to moderately low, cover, and simmer until the chicken is very tender and the sauce is thickened, about 50 minutes.

➤ Stored in a tightly covered container, this will freeze well for up to 3 months. Since it has less liquid than some stews, I don't like to keep it longer.

Chicken Primavera

6 Servings

Chicken with vegetables is a natural pairing, and when it's spring and those vegetables include freshly picked peas and beans and sweet, tender young carrots, so much the better. Of course, at other times of year this stew can be made with frozen peas (add them during the last few minutes). While mushrooms and onions are not necessarily spring crops, I love the earthy note and hint of sweetness that they respectively add. Serve over noodles or with mashed potatoes.

1 (3½-pound) chicken
Salt and freshly ground pepper
2½ tablespoons olive oil
1 cup dry white vermouth
4 tablespoons butter
6 ounces fresh mushrooms, quartered
3 shallots, minced
2½ tablespoons flour
3 cups Rich Chicken Stock (page 232), or 1 (14½-ounce) can
    reduced-sodium broth mixed with 1 cup water
1 teaspoon fresh lemon thyme leaves or ¾ teaspoon dried leaves
⅛ teaspoon cayenne
10 ounces tiny pearl onions, preferably red, peeled (see Note,
    page 15)
2 carrots, peeled and cut into 1 by ⅜-inch sticks
1 cup peas, preferably fresh
1 cup diced (¾-inch) green beans (about ¼ pound)
2 tablespoons chopped basil or parsley

1. Cut the chicken into 10 pieces: 2 drumsticks, 2 thighs, 2 wings with a bit of breast meat attached, and 4 pieces of breast (both sides split crosswise in half). Rinse the chicken pieces and pat dry. Season liberally with salt and pepper. In a large skillet, heat 1½ tablespoons of the oil over moderate heat. Add the chicken in a single layer, in batches if necessary, and cook, turning, until lightly browned, about 7 minutes per batch. Remove to a plate. Drain off all the fat in

the pan and pour in the vermouth. Bring to a boil over high heat, scraping up the brown bits from the bottom of the pan. Set aside.

2. In a large flameproof casserole, melt 2 tablespoons of the butter in the remaining oil over moderately high heat. Add the mushrooms to the pan and cook, stirring, until lightly browned, 3 to 5 minutes. Remove to a bowl.

3. Add the remaining 2 tablespoons butter and the shallots to the pan and cook until softened and fragrant, about 1 minute. Add the flour and cook, stirring, 1 minute longer. Pour in the vermouth from the skillet and bring to a boil. Whisk in the chicken stock and add the thyme and cayenne. Bring to a boil and reduce the heat to moderately low.

4. Return the chicken to the pan along with any juices that have collected on the plate. Add the pearl onions and simmer, partially covered, 20 minutes. Add the carrots, peas, green beans, and mushrooms and simmer, still partially covered, 10 minutes longer, or until the vegetables are just tender.

5. Season with additional salt and pepper to taste. Simmer, uncovered, for 5 minutes. Serve garnished with the basil or parsley.

➤ This dish is best eaten fresh. Stored in a tightly covered container, it can be frozen for up to 6 months, but the carrots and green beans will lose their texture.

Provençal Lemon Chicken with Olives and Garlic

4 to 6 Servings

Y*ou just might feel the Mediterranean sun stream into your kitchen with this savory stew. Serve in a bowl with pasta or rice, crusty toasted bread, and an arugula or watercress and endive salad on the side.*

¼ *pound large green olives*

¼ *pound Kalamata or Gaeta olives*

1 (3½- to 4-pound) chicken

½ *teaspoon salt*

½ *teaspoon freshly ground pepper*

2 teaspoons herbes de Provence

2 tablespoons olive oil

1½ tablespoons extra-virgin olive oil

2 large heads of garlic, separated into cloves and peeled

2 plum tomatoes, peeled, seeded, and chopped or 1 cup drained chopped canned tomatoes

1 tablespoon sherry wine vinegar

¾ *cup dry white wine*

2 cups Brown Chicken Stock (page 233)

1 tablespoon lemon juice

¼ *cup chopped parsley*

1. Bring a medium saucepan of water to a boil. Add all the olives and boil 1 minute. Drain and rinse under cold running water.

2. Rinse the chicken and pat dry. Separate the chicken legs and thighs, cut off the wings, and cut the breast halves crosswise in half; there will be 10 pieces. Trim off all excess fat from the chicken. Season with salt, pepper, and 1 teaspoon of the herbes de Provence.

3. In a large flameproof casserole, heat the 2 tablespoons of olive oil over moderately high heat. Add the chicken in 2 batches and cook, turning, until golden brown, 8 to 10 minutes per batch. Remove the chicken to a platter and pour off the fat from the pan.

4. Add the extra-virgin olive oil to the pan and set over moderate heat. Add the garlic cloves and turn to coat with oil. Cook, stirring, 1 to 2 minutes, until they begin to turn golden. Add the chopped tomatoes and remaining herbes de Provence. Raise the heat to moderately high and cook, stirring often, until the tomatoes are pulpy and some of their liquid is slightly thickened, 2 to 3 minutes. Add the vinegar and cook 30 seconds. Add the wine and boil until reduced by one-third, 1 to 2 minutes.

5. Return the chicken pieces to the pan and add the stock. Cover and simmer 20 minutes. Add the olives and lemon juice. Simmer, partially covered, 15 minutes longer, or until the chicken is tender. Season with salt and pepper to taste. Remove from the heat, cover, and let stand about 10 minutes. Serve garnished with parsley.

➤ The flavors of this stew mellow beautifully if it is reheated the next day. It can be frozen for up to 3 months, but it loses some of its brightness. To freshen, stir in a crushed clove of garlic and 1 teaspoon lemon juice and simmer for a minute or two before serving.

Triple-Mustard Chicken Dijon

6 Servings   This is a wonderful party dish, but it needs something green on top to dress it up. Minced fresh chervil, chives, or parsley are all good choices. Look for the smallest chicken parts you can find, so there will be more pieces. Serve over white or wild rice.

2 pounds skinless chicken breasts on the bone

2 pounds skinless chicken thighs

2 tablespoons butter

1 medium onion, finely chopped

¼ cup Dijon mustard, preferably imported

3 tablespoons honey mustard

2 tablespoons Pommery (coarse grainy) mustard

¾ cup dry white wine, preferably Chardonnay

1½ cups Rich Chicken Stock (page 232) or reduced-sodium canned broth

⅓ cup sour cream

1. Separate the chicken breasts if they are attached and cut each crosswise in half. Trim off any loose fat from all the chicken.

2. In a large flameproof casserole, melt the butter over moderate heat. Add the onion and cook, stirring occasionally, until soft and translucent, about 3 minutes. Add the chicken and cook, turning, until it is no longer pink on the outside, 5 to 7 minutes.

3. In a small bowl, whisk together the 3 mustards. Gradually whisk in the wine. Pour over the chicken and bring to a boil. Add the stock. Partially cover the pan, reduce the heat to moderately low, and simmer 25 to 30 minutes, until the chicken is tender and juicy with no trace of pink near the bone.

4. Remove from the heat, stir in the sour cream, and serve.

➤ Because of the sour cream, which can curdle, it surprised me that this stew not only reheats, but freezes well for up to 3 months. If the sauce does look separated after reheating, remove the pieces of chicken and simply whisk the sauce briefly; it will come together beautifully.

Summer Chicken Ragout
with Sweet Corn, Fresh Tomatoes,
and Cilantro

6 Servings *This is a light stew, with minimal cooking and a thin broth. It is best served freshly made.*

> 2 pounds skinless, boneless chicken breasts
> 4 to 5 ears of fresh sweet corn (to yield 3 cups kernels)
> 3 tablespoons unsalted butter
> 2 medium leeks (white part only) or 2 medium onions, chopped
> 1 or 2 fresh jalapeño or serrano pepper(s), seeded and minced
> 3 cups Rich Chicken Stock (page 232)
> ¾ teaspoon salt
> 1 teaspoon grated lime zest
> ¼ cup fresh lime juice
> 1 large ripe tomato, peeled, seeded, and cut into ½-inch dice
> 3 tablespoons coarsely chopped cilantro or basil

1. Trim any excess fat from the chicken and cut the breast halves crosswise into 1-inch strips. Cut the corn kernels off the cob. With the back of the knife, scrape down the cobs to remove all the corn "cream." Set both the kernels and the corn cream aside.

2. In a large flameproof casserole, melt the butter over moderate heat. Add the leeks and cook, stirring occasionally, until softened and beginning to turn golden, 5 to 7 minutes. Add the jalapeño pepper(s) and cook about 1 minute longer. Stir in the chicken stock, salt, lime zest, and 3 tablespoons of the lime juice. Bring just to a simmer.

3. Add the strips of chicken and all the corn. Cook over moderately low heat until the chicken is just white throughout but still juicy, 5 to 7 minutes. Stir in the diced tomato, remaining 1 tablespoon lime juice, and the cilantro. Serve at once.

➤ This quick, sprightly tasting dish can be reheated, in which case the lime juice and cilantro should be stirred in just before serving, but it is best fresh and is not designed to be frozen.

Ragout of Chicken with Artichokes and Asparagus

4 to 6 Servings **M**any years ago in a chic bistro in
Paris, I enjoyed an immensely savory sauté of chicken in a brown sauce
with artichokes and asparagus. This is my stew version of that dish. While it
is elegant, eating the artichokes may require fingers, which makes it an
excellent choice for a special dinner with good friends.

1 (3½- to 4-pound) chicken
½ teaspoon salt
¼ teaspoon freshly ground pepper
3 tablespoons olive oil
1 tablespoon unsalted butter
1 pound small white pearl onions, peeled (see **Note**, *page 15)*
½ tablespoon flour
⅔ cup dry white wine
3 cups Brown Chicken Stock (page 233)
¼ teaspoon dried thyme leaves
1 tablespoon fresh lemon juice
¾ pound baby artichokes
2 pounds fresh asparagus, cut diagonally into 2-inch pieces

1. Rinse the chicken and pat dry. Cut into 10 serving pieces: 2 drumsticks, 2 thighs, 2 wings with a bit of breast meat attached, and 4 breast pieces (both sides split crosswise in half). Season the chicken pieces with the salt and pepper.

2. In a large flameproof casserole, heat 2 tablespoons of the olive oil over moderately high heat. Add the chicken in a single layer without crowding, in batches if necessary, and cook, turning once, until golden brown, 8 to 10 minutes per batch. As the chicken pieces brown, remove them to a platter. Pour off all fat from the pan.

3. Add the remaining olive oil and the butter to the pan and set over moderately high heat. Add the pearl onions and cook, tossing and stirring often,

until they are golden brown all over, about 8 minutes. Reduce the heat to moderate after about 5 minutes. Remove the onions to a bowl.

4. Add the flour to the fat remaining in the pan. Cook, stirring, 1 minute. Pour in the wine and bring to a boil, scraping up the brown bits from the bottom of the pan. Boil until reduced by half, about 2 minutes. Return the chicken pieces to the pan along with any juices that have collected on the platter. Add the chicken stock, thyme, and half the lemon juice. Simmer 30 minutes.

5. Meanwhile, trim the artichokes: Remove the outer leaves by bending them back and pulling them off; trim the stems and cut off the top third of each artichoke to remove the prickles. Quarter the artichokes lengthwise and scoop out the hairy chokes from the center. Toss the artichoke pieces with the remaining lemon juice. In a large saucepan of boiling salted water, cook the artichokes 5 to 7 minutes, or until just tender. Drain into a colander and rinse under cold running water to stop the cooking.

6. Add the artichokes and the browned onions to the chicken and simmer 15 minutes. In a medium saucepan of boiling salted water, cook the asparagus until tender, about 2 minutes. Drain and rinse under cold running water; drain well. Add to the stew and simmer 5 minutes. Season with additional salt and pepper to taste.

➤ While this stew does freeze acceptably well, the artichokes may darken and the asparagus can loose its texture, so I prefer it freshly made or reheated the next day.

Chicken and Other Poultry Stews

Southwest Chicken Stew with Corn and Cilantro

4 to 6 Servings M*ildly spicy and imbued with the best of the Southwest, this recipe is for your friends who love Mexican food. If you don't have access to pepitas, they can be omitted; the stew will be a little thinner and will lack that extra dimension but will still be tasty. Serve it with rice and Braised Black Beans (see page 92) or refried beans and a tart, crisp salad.*

> 1 (3½- to 4-pound) chicken, cut into 10 serving pieces
> 1 teaspoon ground cumin
> 1 teaspoon dried oregano, preferably Mexican
> 1 teaspoon salt
> ½ teaspoon freshly ground pepper
> 1 pound Anaheim chile peppers
> ¾ pound fresh tomatillos
> ½ cup green pumpkin seeds (see Note)
> 2 cups Rich Chicken Stock (page 232) or reduced-sodium
>   canned broth
> 2½ tablespoons vegetable oil
> 1 medium onion, chopped
> 3 garlic cloves, chopped
> 3 ears of fresh corn
> ⅓ cup crème fraîche or heavy cream
> ⅔ cup chopped cilantro

1. Remove as much skin as possible from the chicken and trim off any excess fat. Season the chicken with the cumin, oregano, salt, and pepper. Set aside while you roast the peppers and tomatillos.

2. Set the peppers and tomatillos over a hot barbecue fire, or under a preheated broiler as close to the heat as possible, and roast, turning, until charred all over, 7 to 10 minutes for the peppers and 3 to 5 minutes for the tomatillos. Place the peppers in a brown paper bag and let stand for 10 minutes. Peel and

chop the tomatillos. Rub the skins off the peppers and remove the stems, seeds, and ribs. Chop the roasted peppers. Set the vegetables aside.

3. In a dry medium skillet, toast the pumpkin seeds over moderate heat, shaking the pan, until they pop, 3 to 4 minutes. Cover the pan if necessary to prevent them from jumping out. In a blender or food processor, puree the pumpkin seeds with 1 cup of the chicken stock.

4. In a large flameproof casserole, heat the oil over moderate heat. Add the onion and garlic and cook, stirring occasionally, until the onion is softened, about 3 minutes. Add the chicken and cook, turning with tongs, until it loses its pink color on the outside, about 5 minutes. Add the remaining chicken stock, pumpkin seed puree, and chopped roasted vegetables. Bring to a simmer, cover, and cook over low heat 45 minutes.

5. Meanwhile, cut the kernels off the corn cobs and with the back of the knife, scrape off all the corn "cream." After the chicken has cooked for 40 minutes, add all the corn to the pot. Stir in the crème fraîche and ⅓ cup of the cilantro and simmer 10 minutes longer. Season the stew with additional salt and pepper to taste. Just before serving, stir in the remaining cilantro.

◇ **Note:** Raw hulled pumpkin seeds are available in health food stores and in Mexican markets, where they are called *pepitas*.

➤ Stored in a tightly covered container, this stew will freeze well for up to 3 months. Because it is very thick, you may have to add a little extra broth when you reheat it, or reheat it in a microwave oven.

Chicken Succotash with Corn, Lima Beans, and Buttermilk

4 to 6 Servings

Big chunks of bright yellow corn, pale green limas, and the pink salt pork make this a pretty stew. I like to serve it in a bowl with a spoon as well as a knife and fork, because the sauce is so savory. The corn can be picked up or cut off the cob. Buttermilk adds a lovely nutty tang at the end, thickening and enriching the stew without the fat of heavy cream. It must not be boiled, though, or it will curdle.

1 (3½- to 4-pound) chicken

¼ cup plus 1 tablespoon flour

½ teaspoon salt

½ teaspoon freshly ground pepper

1 teaspoon dried thyme leaves

¼ teaspoon cayenne

2 tablespoons vegetable oil

¼ pound salt pork, blanched and cut into ¼-inch lardons

2 medium onions, cut into ½-inch dice

3 cups Rich Chicken Stock (page 232)

1 cup milk (use 2 percent; 1 percent or skim will be too thin)

2 large red potatoes, peeled and cut into ¾-inch dice

3 ears of fresh corn, cut into 1-inch pieces

1½ cups thawed frozen baby lima beans

1 cup buttermilk

1. Rinse the chicken and pat dry. Cut into 10 serving pieces: 2 drumsticks, 2 thighs, 2 wings, and 4 pieces of breast (both sides cut crosswise in half).

2. In a shallow bowl, mix together ¼ cup of the flour with the salt, pepper, ½ teaspoon of the thyme, and the cayenne. Dredge the chicken in the seasoned flour to coat; shake off any excess.

3. In a large flameproof casserole, heat the oil. Add the salt pork and cook over moderate heat, stirring occasionally, until the salt pork is golden and lightly browned around the edges, about 5 minutes. With a slotted spoon, remove to paper towels to drain.

4. Add the chicken to the fat in the pan in 2 batches and cook, turning, until golden brown, about 7 minutes per batch. As the chicken is browned, remove it. Pour off all but 2 tablespoons fat from the pan.

5. Add the onions to the pan and cook, stirring often, until softened and golden, 3 to 5 minutes. Sprinkle the remaining 1 tablespoon flour over the onions and cook, stirring, 1 minute. Add the stock, milk, and remaining ½ teaspoon thyme and bring to a boil.

6. Return the chicken and salt pork to the casserole. Bring to a simmer, reduce the heat to moderately low, partially cover, and cook 10 minutes. Add the potatoes and cook 10 minutes longer. Skim off as much fat as you can from the top of the sauce.

7. Add the corn to the casserole and cook, stirring once or twice, until the corn is almost tender, about 10 minutes. Add the limas and simmer 2 minutes. Season with additional salt and pepper to taste.

8. Just before serving, remove from the heat and stir in the buttermilk.

➤ This dish can be reheated the next day if you are careful not to boil the buttermilk; if you do, it will still taste good, but it will look curdled. I do not recommend freezing it.

Turkey Fajita Pie

8 Servings

Here turkey is cooked over high heat, preferably in a cast-iron skillet, to obtain as much browning as possible first before the liquids are added. This is an easy do-ahead recipe for informal company. It can be prepared completely ahead, be refrigerated or frozen, and baked at the last minute. Serve with guacamole and sour cream on the side.

3 pounds lean ground turkey

1½ tablespoons chili powder

2 teaspoons ground cumin

1 teaspoon dried Mexican oregano

1 teaspoon salt

3 tablespoons vegetable oil

2 medium onions, coarsely chopped

1 green bell pepper, cut into ⅜-inch dice

1 red bell pepper, cut into ⅜-inch dice

1 (14½-ounce) can reduced-sodium chicken broth

1 (14½-ounce) can recipe-ready diced tomatoes, with their juice

1½ tablespoons sherry wine vinegar

1 tablespoon lime juice

1 tablespoon Worcestershire sauce

1 (16-ounce) can corn kernels, drained

1 (2-ounce) can sliced ripe olives, drained

3 tablespoons finely chopped pickled jalapeño peppers, plus
    2 to 3 teaspoons of the juice

2 tablespoons yellow cornmeal

Cheddar Puff Crust (recipe follows)

1. In a medium bowl, use your hands to blend the turkey well with the chili powder, cumin, oregano, and salt. Heat a wok or large cast-iron skillet over high heat. Add 1 tablespoon of the oil and swirl to coat the pan. Add the seasoned turkey and cook, stirring often, until browned, 5 to 7 minutes.

2. In a large flameproof casserole, heat the remaining 2 tablespoons oil over moderate heat. Add the onions and cook, stirring occasionally, until they are

golden and beginning to brown around the edges, 5 to 7 minutes. Add the bell peppers and cook 3 minutes to soften slightly.

3. Add the chicken broth, tomatoes with their juice, vinegar, lime juice, Worcestershire, corn, olives, and jalapeño peppers with juice. Add the turkey to the casserole along with any juices that have collected on the plate. Stir to mix well. Partially cover and simmer 20 minutes. Gradually sprinkle the cornmeal over the stew as you stir it in. Simmer 5 minutes, until slightly thickened.

4. Preheat the oven to 425 degrees F. Turn the turkey fajita mixture into a large shallow (8 by 12-inch) baking dish. Cover with the Cheddar Puff Crust.

5. Bake 25 to 35 minutes, or until the pastry is puffed and browned and the turkey mixture is bubbling hot. If the pastry browns too quickly, tent with foil during the last 10 minutes or so of cooking.

➤ This dish can be prepared in advance through Step 4 and refrigerated for up to 2 days or frozen for up to 2 months. Bake just before serving.

Cheddar Puff Crust

Makes a single crust large enough to cover an 8- by 12-inch rectangle

1 (9½-inch) square of frozen puff pastry (half a 17½-ounce package)

½ cup grated Romano cheese

1½ cups finely shredded sharp Cheddar cheese

1 egg, beaten with 2 teaspoons water

1. Thaw the pastry as directed on the package. Sprinkle the Romano cheese over a flat work surface and use it, instead of flour, to roll out the pastry into a 12-inch square.

2. Sprinkle about half the Cheddar cheese over the pastry and fold the square in half to make a 12- by 6-inch rectangle. Sprinkle the remaining cheese over the pastry and fold again to make a 6-inch square.

3. Roll out the pastry into an 8- by 12-inch rectangle. After setting over the filling, brush the pastry with the egg wash before baking.

Thanksgiving Turkey Potpie

8 Servings

It's not often you can feed eight people with 1½ pounds of meat, and it's not often you might want to, but the day after Thanksgiving might well be one of those occasions. All this twice-baked stew needs to complete the meal is some cranberry sauce, or perhaps a cranberry chutney, left over from the same holiday feast.

1½ pounds cooked turkey meat

1 pound roasted yellow onions or boiled tiny white pearl onions

1 pound roasted or boiled potatoes

½ pound cooked carrots (about 3 medium)

½ pound cooked parsnips (about 4 medium)

1 cup cooked or thawed frozen peas

2 tablespoons butter

1 tablespoon olive oil

1 medium onion, cut into ½-inch dice

1 large celery rib with leaves, cut into ½-inch dice

¼ cup flour

3 cups turkey stock, Rich Chicken Stock (page 232),
*   or reduced-sodium canned broth*

½ teaspoon dried thyme leaves

½ teaspoon crumbled sage

Salt

Freshly ground black pepper

Old-Fashioned Bread Stuffing (recipe follows) or 6 cups leftover
*   stuffing from your Thanksgiving turkey or other simple*
*   bread stuffing*

1. Cut or tear the turkey into large chunks.

2. Cut the roasted yellow onions into 1-inch wedges; if using pearl onions, leave them whole. Cut the potatoes, carrots, and parsnips into 1-inch chunks. Combine all these ingredients with the turkey and peas in a shallow 3- to 4-quart baking dish.

3. In a large skillet or flameproof casserole, melt the butter in the oil over moderate heat. Add the diced onion and celery and cook, stirring occasionally, until the onion begins to color, about 7 minutes.

4. Preheat the oven to 375 degrees F.

5. Sprinkle the flour over the onions and celery and cook, stirring, 1 minute. Stir in the stock and bring to a boil, stirring, until evenly thickened. Season with the thyme, sage, and salt and pepper to taste. Pour the sauce over the turkey and vegetables and stir gently to mix.

6. Spoon the stuffing over the turkey stew and bake 25 to 30 minutes, or until the stew is bubbling hot and the stuffing is lightly browned on top.

➤ This is a leftover dish to begin with, so I wouldn't try to freeze it, but you can prepare it hours ahead and bake it at the last moment.

Old-Fashioned Bread Stuffing

6 to 8 Servings

1 pound soft Italian or firm-textured white bread, cut into
   ¾-inch cubes
2 tablespoons olive oil
2 medium onions, coarsely chopped
1 celery rib with leaves, coarsely chopped
⅓ pound fresh sausage meat
2 tablespoons chopped fresh parsley
¾ teaspoon crumbled dried sage
½ teaspoon dried thyme leaves
½ teaspoon salt
¼ teaspoon freshly ground pepper
2 eggs, lightly beaten
About 1 cup turkey or chicken stock

1. Preheat the oven to 325 degrees F.

2. Spread out the bread cubes on a baking sheet and bake 40 to 45 minutes, shaking the pan occasionally to toss them, until they are dried out. If the bread is stale to begin with, it will take less time. Transfer to a large bowl.

3. In a large skillet, heat the olive oil over moderate heat. Add the onions and celery and cook, stirring occasionally, until soft but not brown, 3 to 5 minutes. Add the sausage and cook, breaking up any large lumps, until the meat is lightly browned, 5 to 7 minutes. Scrape the contents of the skillet over the bread.

4. Add the parsley, sage, thyme, salt, pepper, and eggs and toss lightly to mix. Gradually add just enough stock while stirring the stuffing to moisten lightly.

5. Use as a topping or to stuff a large chicken or small turkey, or turn into a baking dish and bake separately.

Duck with Olives

4 Servings

Many years ago I tasted a fabulous duck with olives at a Parisian bistro called Chez Allard, which at the time was a starred Michelin restaurant. This is an easy stewed version of the dish. It is also one stews that improves upon sitting overnight.

1 (4½- to 5-pound) duckling
Salt
Freshly ground pepper
2 tablespoons olive oil
1 medium onion, finely chopped
3 garlic cloves, minced
½ cup dry Madeira
¾ cup dry white wine
1 pound fresh plum tomatoes, peeled, seeded, and
    chopped, or 1 (28-ounce) can Italian peeled tomatoes,
    drained and chopped
2½ cups Brown Chicken Stock (page 233)
10 ounces tiny white pearl onions, peeled (see Note, page 15)
1 teaspoon herbes de Provence
1 bay leaf
1½ cups pitted colossal green olives, preferably from the deli
    section of your supermarket (about 10 ounces)
2 teaspoons cornstarch
1 tablespoon sherry wine vinegar
1½ tablespoons chopped parsley

1. Cut the duck into serving pieces. Separate each wing with a little of the breast meat attached. Cut off the 2 legs and thighs together. Cut each breast crosswise in half as best you can through the bone. Cut off the tail, but use the back as well, because there are a couple of nice nuggets of meat on either side of the backbone. Pull off as much skin as you can and trim off all excess fat. Season the duck liberally with salt and pepper.

2. In a large flameproof casserole, heat the olive oil over moderately high heat. Add the duck in 2 batches and cook, turning, until lightly browned, about 5 minutes per batch. Remove to a plate.

3. Add the chopped onion to the casserole and cook, stirring occasionally, until softened, about 3 minutes. Add the garlic and cook 1 minute longer. Pour in the Madeira and the white wine. Bring to a boil, scraping up the brown bits from the bottom of the pan. Boil until reduced by half, 2 to 3 minutes.

4. Stir the tomatoes into the casserole. Return the duck to the pan, along with any juices that have collected on the plate. Pour in the stock and add the pearl onions, herbes de Provence, and bay leaf. Cover, reduce the heat to low, and simmer 25 minutes.

5. Meanwhile, bring a medium saucepan of water to a simmer. Add the olives and simmer 3 minutes. Drain the olives into a colander.

6. Add the olives to the duck in the casserole. Continue to simmer, partially covered, until the duck is tender, 20 to 30 minutes longer. Remove the duck and olives to a serving dish and cover to keep warm. Skim any fat off the liquid in the pan. Remove and discard the bay leaf. Boil over high heat to reduce slightly, about 3 minutes. Dissolve the cornstarch in 1 tablespoon water and stir into the sauce. Boil about 2 minutes, stirring, until thickened and clear. Stir in the vinegar. Season the sauce with additional salt and pepper to taste. Pour over the duck and olives, garnish with the parsley, and serve.

➤ This dish improves in flavor when left to stand for a few hours at room temperature or in the refrigerator overnight and reheated. Because of the large olives and tiny onions, both of which would suffer in texture, I do not like to freeze this stew.

Sweet and Sour Duck
with Cherries

4 Servings

This is an easy company dish that needs only wild rice and perhaps some buttered broccoli to accompany it. I remove the skin from the duck because I want as little fat as possible in the dish. The duck also cooks much faster this way.

1 (5-pound) duck

1¾ teaspoons coarse (kosher) salt

1 teaspoon coarsely cracked black pepper

1 teaspoon dried thyme leaves

½ teaspoon ground allspice

1½ tablespoons cognac or Armagnac

2 tablespoons olive oil

4 large shallots, finely chopped

1 cup port

2 cups dry red wine

2 tablespoons butter

2 cups Brown Chicken Stock (page 233)

1 cinnamon stick

3 whole cloves

1 teaspoon black peppercorns

1 bay leaf

2 tablespoons red wine vinegar

1 tablespoon Dijon mustard

1 (16-ounce) can sweet cherries in syrup, syrup reserved

2 teaspoons cornstarch

1 (16-ounce) can tart cherries in water, drained

2 to 3 teaspoons fresh lemon juice

1. Cut the duck into serving pieces. Separate each wing with a little of the breast meat attached. Cut off the 2 legs and thighs together. Cut each breast crosswise in half as best you can through the bone. Cut off the tail, but use the back as well, because there are a couple of nice nuggets of meat on either side of the

backbone. Pull off as much skin as you can and trim off all excess fat. Season the duck with 1½ teaspoons salt, ½ teaspoon pepper, ½ teaspoon thyme, and the allspice. Sprinkle the cognac over the duck and drizzle on 1 tablespoon of the olive oil. Set aside at room temperature for 1 hour.

2. In a nonreactive medium saucepan, combine the shallots and ¾ cup of the port. Boil until the port is reduced to a couple of tablespoons. Pour in the red wine and boil until it is reduced by half. Remove from the heat and set aside.

3. Remove the duck from its marinade and pat dry. In a large flameproof casserole, melt the butter in the remaining 1 tablespoon oil. Add the duck pieces in 2 batches and cook over moderate heat, turning, until lightly browned, about 5 minutes per batch. Remove to a plate.

4. Pour the wine reduction into the pan and bring to a boil, scraping up any brown bits from the bottom of the pan. Add the stock and the duck along with any juices that have collected on the plate.

5. Tie the cinnamon stick, cloves, peppercorns, bay leaf, and remaining ½ teaspoon thyme in cheesecloth and add to the pan.

6. Whisk the vinegar and mustard into the reserved cherry syrup and add to the pan. Season with the remaining ¼ teaspoon salt and ½ teaspoon pepper. Bring to a boil, cover, reduce the heat to low, and simmer 45 to 60 minutes, or until the duck is tender.

7. Remove the duck to a bowl. Skim off as much fat as possible from the top of the sauce. Boil the sauce until it is intense and reduced to about 2½ cups, about 5 minutes. Remove and discard the spice bag.

8. Dissolve the cornstarch in the remaining ¼ cup port and stir into the sauce. Bring to a boil, stirring until smooth and clear, about 2 minutes. Add the cherries to the pan. Stir in the lemon juice and season with additional salt and pepper to taste. Return the duck to the pan and heat through before serving.

➤ Stored in a tightly covered container, this stew will freeze well for up to 3 months.

Pheasant Stewed in White Wine with Forest Mushrooms

6 to 8 Servings **P**heasant is one of the great treats of *the fall and early winter, when you can usually find it in good butcher shops. This exceptionally savory recipe is from The Settler's Inn in Hawley, Pennsylvania, a charming country restaurant with rooms, where the chefs follow the admirable new American culinary trend of cooking with ingredients that are close to the local land. Serve with noodles or wild rice.*

1 large pheasant (3 to 3½ pounds)

1 teaspoon salt

¾ teaspoon freshly ground pepper

¼ pound bacon, cut into ¼-inch-wide strips

¼ cup flour

2 cups Rich Chicken Stock (page 232) or reduced-sodium canned broth

2 medium onions, chopped

4 carrots, diced

½ pound fresh shiitakes, cèpes, morels, cremini, or other woodsy mushroom, trimmed and halved or quartered

3 garlic cloves, chopped

2 bay leaves

1½ teaspoons dried thyme leaves

Pinch of cayenne

1 (14½-ounce) can Italian peeled tomatoes, chopped, juice reserved

1 cup dry white wine

2 tablespoons balsamic vinegar

1. Preheat the oven to 350 degrees F.

2. Cut the pheasant into 8 serving pieces: 2 legs with thighs, 2 wings with a small piece of breast meat attached, and 4 pieces of breast (cut both sides crosswise in half). Season with half the salt and pepper.

3. In a large skillet, cook the bacon over moderate heat until it is crisp, about 5 minutes. Remove the bacon to paper towels. Leave the fat in the pan.

4. Dredge the pheasant in flour. Add it to the fat in the skillet in a single layer without crowding, in batches if necessary, and sauté over moderately high heat, turning, until brown, about 7 minutes per batch. Transfer the pheasant to a stewpot, pour in the stock, cover, braise in the oven 1 hour.

5. Meanwhile, add the onions and carrots to the fat remaining in the skillet. Cook over moderate heat, stirring occasionally, 3 minutes. Add the mushrooms and garlic, raise the heat to moderately high, and sauté 5 minutes longer. Add the bay leaves, thyme, cayenne, and remaining salt and pepper. Cook, stirring, 1 minute, then add the tomatoes with their juice, the wine, and the vinegar.

6. After 1 hour, for easier serving, remove the pheasant from its stock. As soon as it is cool enough to handle, pull off the meat and discard the skin and bones. Cut the meat into bite-size pieces. Add the tomato mixture in the skillet to the pheasant stock. Return the pheasant to the casserole. Stir in the reserved bacon. Return to the oven for 30 minutes longer or simmer on top of the stove for 30 to 45 minutes, until the flavors are nicely mellowed. Remove and discard the bay leaves. Skim the fat off the top, or refrigerate the stew overnight (it improves upon standing) and scrape the congealed fat off the top the next day.

➤ This stew reheats very nicely, and stored in a tightly covered container, it will freeze well for up to 6 months.

Rabbit Stew Dijonnaise

4 Servings *Rabbit is a mild-tasting, very light meat that is rather hard to come by in this country. Look for it fresh at good butchers and in the frozen section of your supermarket in packages, where it is liable to be labeled "rabbit meat," signaling, I suppose, that you needn't worry about encountering a head or a tail when you open the box. While rabbit is not technically poultry, I put it here because in its effect, it lies somewhere between chicken and veal. Rabbit makes wonderful stew because it imbibes the flavor of its sauce; here it is mingled with Dijon mustard and vinegar in a stew-like variation of a classic French sauté. Serve with mashed potatoes or noodles.*

1 (3- to 3½-pound) rabbit

¼ cup Dijon mustard

3 garlic cloves, minced

3 tablespoons red wine vinegar

4½ tablespoons butter

1 tablespoon vegetable oil

1 cup dry white wine

3 cups Brown Chicken Stock (page 233) or Rich Chicken Stock
    (page 232)

¾ teaspoon dried thyme leaves

1 bay leaf

3 medium carrots, peeled and roll-cut into ¾-inch lengths
    (see page 77, Step 4)

10 ounces tiny white pearl onions, peeled (see Note, page 15)

½ pound mushrooms, halved or quartered

3 tablespoons flour

2 tablespoons heavy cream

Salt

Freshly ground black pepper

¼ cup chopped parsley

1. Cut up the rabbit on the bone into 2- to 3-inch pieces.

2. In a small bowl, blend 3 tablespoons of the mustard, the garlic, and 2 tablespoons of the vinegar. Smear all over the rabbit pieces and let stand at room temperature at least 30 minutes and up to 1½ hours.

3. In a large flameproof casserole, melt 2 tablespoons of the butter in the oil. Add the rabbit pieces with their marinade clinging to them in batches without crowding and sauté over moderately high heat, turning, until lightly colored, about 5 minutes per batch. Remove the rabbit pieces to a plate. (If the bits of garlic begin to burn, reduce the heat to moderate.)

4. Pour the wine into the pan and bring to a boil, scraping up any brown bits from the bottom of the pan. Boil until reduced by half. Add the stock, thyme, and bay leaf. Return the rabbit to the pot, partially cover, and simmer 1 hour.

5. Add the carrots, onions, and mushrooms and simmer 20 to 30 minutes longer, or until the rabbit and all the vegetables are tender. With a slotted spoon, remove the rabbit and vegetables to a serving dish and cover to keep warm. Remove and discard the bay leaf.

6. Blend the remaining butter with the flour to make a paste. Gradually stir into the sauce and bring to a boil. Boil until thickened, about 2 minutes. In a small bowl, whisk the cream with the remaining 1 tablespoon each mustard and vinegar. Whisk into the sauce in the pan until well blended. Season with salt and pepper to taste. Stir in the parsley, pour over the rabbit, and serve.

➤ Rabbit, like chicken, refreezes well. Stored in a tightly covered container, this stew can be frozen for up to 6 months, though the carrots tend to get a bit mealy.

Beef, Veal, and Venison Stews

eef makes the quintessential stew: a bowl of steaming glossy brown gravy supporting beautifully browned cubes of meat, mixed with chunks of carrots, potatoes, turnips, green beans, and what have you. Covered with dollops of dumplings or served over mashed potatoes or noodles, it is heartwarming food, always welcome, always delicious.

Add bacon and wine and you have Tangy Cabernet Beef. Add brown beer and onions and you have Carbonnade Flamande. Add sherry and tomato paste and you have Cuban Picadillo. It is not news that most cooks for decades have chosen chuck and sometimes even brisket as the prime cuts for stew; they are inexpensive and fatty. Fat does carry flavor, and with long enough cooking, it melts down into an unctuous, tender texture. Nonetheless, I chose to make most of these beef stews with top or bottom round, which is both leaner and consequently drier. On the plus side, I find that round holds its shape with repeated reheating — a big bonus with stews, many of which freeze well — whereas chuck can dissolve into long, stringy strands. And round takes less time to cook than chuck, which is tougher. The

loss of flavor from fat is compensated for by adding extra flavor to the stews — in the form of wine, or more herbs and spices or other tasty ingredients, such as sun-dried tomatoes, olives, dried fruits, etc.—and moistness can be added by letting the meat cool in the stew and then reheating it.

Veal is young beef — lighter in color and in fat content, silkier in texture and milder in flavor. It creates marvelous stews, since its high proportion of collagen melts into a naturally thickened sauce with extremely pleasant body and flavor. Along with a classic creamy blanquette and a couple of recipes that utilize veal shanks, I've included two authentic Roman dishes that make the most of this delicate meat: Stufatino alla Romano, a simple and irresistible stew of fresh tomatoes, red wine, and marjoram, and Spezzatino of Veal with Fennel, delicately flavored with the aniselike seed.

I've included venison in this chapter as well, because though it is a dark red meat, like both beef and lamb, its flavor is much closer to beef, and bottom round can be substituted successfully in many venison recipes. As this game becomes more widely bred for eating, it is showing up in more and more butcher shops. Mine comes from the *wild, but its flavor and texture are much the same as the meat that is bred on ranches. Venison demands marinating and long, slow cooking with hearty ingredients. Here are two ways to try it: an elegant Venison Stew with Armagnac and Prunes and a hearty Venison Chili with Black Beans and Roasted Peppers, perfect for any party.*

Beef Stew with Roasted Garlic, Mushrooms, and Potatoes

6 to 8 Servings
An old-fashioned, meal-in-a-bowl is *updated by roasting whole heads of garlic, new potatoes, and mushrooms before adding them to the simmering stew, for a depth of flavor that's quite contemporary. While the preparation time here looks daunting, the entire stew can be made days or weeks in advance through Step 5 and reheated or frozen; the vegetables can be roasted several hours before serving and set aside at room temperature; and the whole can be combined shortly before serving. All this needs is a salad, some good bread, and a great bottle of red wine.*

3½ to 4 pounds beef chuck, trimmed and cut into 2-inch cubes

2 medium onions, sliced

2 medium carrots, peeled and sliced

2 garlic cloves, smashed, plus 2 whole heads of garlic

2 cups dry red wine

4 sprigs of parsley

1 bay leaf

1 teaspoon dried thyme leaves

1 teaspoon coarsely cracked black pepper

¼ pound bacon

3 to 4 tablespoons olive oil

¼ cup flour

1½ teaspoons salt

2 cups Simple Meat Stock (page 234)

2 tablespoons tomato paste

1 teaspoon sugar

1½ pounds tiny red potatoes, scrubbed

1 pound medium whole mushrooms, stem ends trimmed slightly

¾ pound green beans

1. Place the beef in a large bowl. Add the onions, carrots, garlic, wine, parsley, bay leaf, thyme, and cracked pepper. Marinate at room temperature, turning the meat occasionally, 4 to 6 hours, or refrigerate overnight.

2. In a medium pot of simmering water, blanch the bacon 3 minutes. Drain and pat dry. Cut the bacon crosswise into ⅜-inch-wide strips.

3. In a large flameproof casserole, heat 2 tablespoons of the oil over moderate heat. Add the bacon and cook until lightly browned, 3 to 5 minutes. Remove with a slotted spoon and set aside.

4. Drain the beef, reserving the marinade and vegetables separately; pat the meat dry. Save the bay leaf; discard the parsley sprigs.

5. In a shallow bowl, mix the flour with the salt and ½ teaspoon freshly ground pepper. Dredge the meat in the seasoned flour, shaking any excess back into the bowl. Add the meat to the pan in batches and cook over moderately high heat, turning, until browned all over, about 7 minutes per batch. Remove with a slotted spoon and set aside.

6. Add the onions and carrots from the marinade to the pan and cook, stirring, until softened, about 5 minutes. Sprinkle the remaining seasoned flour over the vegetables and cook, stirring, 1 minute. Pour in the reserved marinade liquid and the stock. Add the bay leaf. Stir in the tomato paste and sugar. Return the meat to the pan and bring to a simmer. Cover, reduce the heat to low, and simmer 2 to 2½ hours, until the meat is fork tender. Remove and discard the bay leaf.

7. Meanwhile, preheat the oven to 375 degrees F.

8. Cut the tops off the garlic heads and brush with a little olive oil. Wrap in foil and roast 40 to 45 minutes, or until sweet and tender. Set aside to cool. Increase the oven temperature to 425 degrees F.

9. Toss the potatoes and mushrooms in the remaining olive oil separately. Arrange the potatoes in a single layer on a baking sheet and season with salt and pepper. Roast 20 minutes. Turn the potatoes and arrange the mushrooms in an empty area of the baking pan. Roast 25 minutes longer, or until the potatoes are tender and the mushrooms are lightly browned.

10. In a large saucepan of boiling salted water, cook the green beans until tender, 5 to 7 minutes. Drain and rinse under cold running water; drain well.

11. Remove all the individual garlic cloves from their skins. Mash half of them and stir into the stew liquid. Add the remaining whole roasted garlic cloves and the potatoes, mushrooms with any juices, and the green beans to the beef stew. Heat through for 2 to 3 minutes and serve.

➤ While this dish reheats very well after being refrigerated for up to 3 days, I don't like to freeze it, because the potatoes can become mealy and the green beans lose their texture and color.

Old-Fashioned Beef Stew with Coffee and Buttermilk Dumplings

6 to 8 Servings *What's old is new, and what's comforting is back. You won't taste the coffee here, but it adds a extra dimension of flavor to the sauce and nice depth to the color. Steamed dumplings remain soft, but they should be cooked through and light as air.*

2½ to 3 pounds beef chuck or round, cut into 1- to 1½ -inch cubes
⅓ cup flour
1 teaspoon salt
½ teaspoon freshly ground pepper
3 tablespoons bacon drippings or vegetable oil
4 cups Simple Meat Stock (page 234)
1 cup strongly brewed coffee
6 medium onions, peeled and quartered
5 carrots, peeled and cut diagonally into 2-inch pieces
4 large red or white potatoes, peeled and cut into
*   1½ -inch chunks*
6 small white turnips, peeled and quartered
Buttermilk Dumplings (recipe follows)

1. Dredge the beef in the flour, which has been mixed with the salt and pepper. Shake off and reserve any excess.

2. In a large flameproof casserole, heat the bacon drippings. Add the beef to the pan in two batches and cook, turning, until browned, 5 to 7 minutes per batch.

3. Return all the beef to the pan. Add the stock, coffee, and onions, cover, and simmer over low heat 30 minutes. Add the carrots, potatoes, and turnips and continue to simmer, covered, 1 to 1½ hours longer, or until the beef is tender.

4. Prepare Buttermilk Dumplings through Step 1. Uncover the stew and bring to a boil. Drop the dumplings by spoonfuls over the stew, setting them on pieces of meat and vegetables, rather than right in the liquid. Cover and cook over moderate heat for 10 to 15 minutes, until the dumplings are cooked through.

5. With a slotted spoon, remove the beef, vegetables, and dumplings to a serving dish. Stir a couple of tablespoons of water into the reserved seasoned flour and stir that into the boiling liquid in the pot. Boil, stirring, for about 2 minutes, until thickened. Pour around the meat, vegetables, and dumplings.

➤ If you plan to make this dish ahead, prepare it only through Step 3. Add the dumplings after reheating. If you have leftovers, refrigerate the stew and dumplings separately. Bring the stew to a boil, then top with the leftover dumplings and steam for about 5 minutes to reheat them. They will taste fine, though they will be heavier than when freshly made. Because of the dumplings and the root vegetables, which tend to lose their texture, I do not freeze this stew.

Buttermilk Dumplings

These work well in almost any old-fashioned beef or chicken stew. Be sure to make the dough just before you use it, and try to set the dumplings on solid pieces of meat or chunks of vegetables so they don't get soggy.

> *2 cups flour, preferably a soft wheat flour such as White Lily*
> *1½ teaspoons baking powder*
> *1 teaspoon baking soda*
> *¾ teaspoon salt*
> *1½ tablespoons solid vegetable shortening*
> *1 cup buttermilk*

1. In a medium bowl, sift together the flour, baking powder, baking soda, and salt. Cut in the shortening until it is the size of small peas. Mix in the buttermilk until blended. The dough should be soft.

2. Drop at once on top of a simmering stew, placing the dough on top of solid ingredients rather than directly in liquid. Cover and steam 10 to 15 minutes, until the dumplings are cooked through.

Barbecued Beef Stew
with Cheddared Corn Pudding

8 Servings *With its zesty barbecue sauce, this is gutsy party food, which reheats well for easy do-ahead entertaining. Serve a cool salad or Sautéed Collards and Kale (page 119) on the side.*

3½ pounds trimmed beef chuck, cut into 1½-inch chunks

1 teaspoon salt

½ teaspoon freshly ground pepper

3 tablespoons vegetable oil

3 medium onions, chopped

12 ounces beer

½ cup plus 2 tablespoons cider vinegar

½ cup ketchup

3 tablespoons dark brown sugar

1½ tablespoons Worcestershire sauce

2 teaspoons ground cumin

1 teaspoon dry mustard

¾ teaspoon dried marjoram

1 dried chipotle chile

Cheddared Corn Pudding (recipe follows), prepared through Step 2

1. Preheat the oven to 325 degrees F. Season the meat with the salt and pepper.

2. In a large flameproof casserole, heat the oil over moderately high heat. Add the meat in batches without crowding and sauté, turning, until browned all over, about 7 minutes per batch. As the meat is browned, remove it to a plate.

3. Add the onions to the casserole and cook, stirring often, until golden and beginning to brown, about 7 minutes. Return the meat to the pan along with any juices that have collected on the plate. Add the beer, cider vinegar, ketchup, brown sugar, Worcestershire sauce, cumin, mustard, marjoram, and chipotle chile. Bring just to a boil, cover, and transfer to the oven.

4. Bake the stew for 2 to 2½ hours, or until the meat is fork tender and beginning to fall apart. Remove from the oven, but increase the oven temperature to 350 degrees F.

5. With a slotted spoon, remove the meat to a bowl. Skim all excess fat from the top of the stew. Fish out the chipotle chile. Tear off and discard the stem end and puree the chile in a blender or food processor with about 1 cup of the cooking liquid. Stir the chile puree back into the stew. If the sauce is thin, boil uncovered, stirring often and skimming once or twice, until thickened slightly, 5 to 7 minutes. Return the beef to the stew. (The recipe improves if made a day or two in advance. Let cool, then cover and refrigerate. If made ahead, turn off the oven after removing the stew. Preheat the stew and preheat the oven to 350 degrees F. before proceeding.)

6. Turn the barbecued beef and sauce into a 10-by 14-inch (or 11 by 13-inch) casserole about 3 inches deep. Spoon the corn pudding on top and spread to even. Bake 45 to 55 minutes, or until the corn pudding is golden on top, lightly browned around the edges, and just set in the center.

➤ This dish can be completely finished and refrigerated for up to 2 days before being reheated. Prepared through Step 6 and stored in a tightly covered container, the beefy part of this stew will freeze well for up to 3 months. The corn pudding tends to separate if it is frozen, though the flavor remains good.

Cheddared Corn Pudding

8 Servings

> *3 eggs*
>
> *2 cans (16 ounces each) cream-style corn*
>
> *⅛ teaspoon cayenne*
>
> *3 tablespoons butter, melted*
>
> *1½ cups buttermilk*
>
> *⅔ cup saltine cracker crumbs (from 18 crackers)*
>
> *½ cup cornmeal*
>
> *¾ teaspoon baking powder*
>
> *½ teaspoon baking soda*
>
> *1½ cups shredded sharp Cheddar cheese*

1. Preheat the oven to 350 degrees F.

2. In a large bowl, beat the eggs with a fork until blended. Beat in the creamed corn, cayenne, melted butter, buttermilk, cracker crumbs, cornmeal, baking powder, and baking soda until well blended. Stir in the cheese.

3. Turn the pudding into a buttered 2- to 3-quart baking dish (11 by 13) about 2 inches deep. Bake 45 minutes, or until the pudding is lightly browned around the edges and the center is just set. Let stand 5 to 10 minutes before dishing out, to allow the pudding to set up.

Bigos

8 Servings **W.** *Peter Prestcott,* Food & Wine *magazine's entertaining and special projects director, makes the best bigos, a traditional Polish beef and sausage stew with sauerkraut and caraway, that I have ever tasted. This is his recipe. The dish really should be made a day ahead and allowed to sit in the refrigerator overnight. If you do so, the flavor improves dramatically. Peter usually makes this for a party in twice this quantity. Even if the recipe is doubled, 1½ ounces of the mushrooms will be plenty.*

1 ounce dried imported mushrooms
2 pounds fresh sauerkraut
¼ pound salt pork, cut into ½-inch dice
1⅔ cups dry red wine
1 (6-ounce) can tomato paste
3 garlic cloves, finely chopped
1 bay leaf
1½ pounds smoked kielbasa sausage, cut into ½-inch slices
½ cup vodka
2 tablespoons butter
1 tablespoon olive oil
2 pounds trimmed beef chuck, cut into 1-inch cubes
1 tablespoon caraway seeds
½ pound kosher dill pickles, coarsely chopped
Sour cream (optional)

1. In a small heatproof bowl, soak the mushrooms in 2 cups boiling water for 20 minutes, until softened. Strain the liquid into a small bowl, squeezing the mushrooms to release as much liquid as possible; reserve the liquid. Coarsely chop the mushrooms.

2. Rinse the sauerkraut well in a colander under cold running water. Drain and squeeze out as much water as possible with your hands.

3. In a small saucepan of boiling water, cook the salt pork for 5 minutes. Drain and rinse briefly under cold water.

4. In a large flameproof casserole, combine the chopped mushrooms, mushroom liquid, sauerkraut, salt pork, wine, tomato paste, garlic, and bay leaf. Cover and simmer slowly over low heat for 2 hours.

5. Add the sausage and cook, covered, for 10 minutes. Increase the heat to moderate and add the vodka. Avert your face and ignite the vodka with a match. Cook, shaking the pan, until the flames subside. Remove from the heat, cover, and set aside.

6. In a large skillet, melt the butter in the oil over high heat. Add half the beef and half the caraway seeds; cook, stirring occasionally, until browned, about 5 minutes. Transfer to the sauerkraut mixture. Repeat with the remaining meat and caraway seeds. Add the browned meat and any juices in the pan to the sauerkraut mixture.

7. Cover and cook over low heat for 1½ hours, or until the beef is tender. (If possible, let cook, then cover and refrigerate overnight before reheating.) Just before serving, remove and discard the bay leaf and stir in the chopped pickles. Pass a bowl of sour cream on the side.

➤ As mentioned in the headnote, this stew reheats beautifully. Stored in a tightly covered container, it will freeze well for up to 3 months.

Tangy Cabernet Beef with Bacon and Onions

6 to 8 Servings

While chuck has more flavor, bottom round is leaner, and it holds its shape much better after a long marinade and cooking. In fact, it withstands reheating well, and so is my first choice for this sort of long-simmering stew. While the total time for this recipe adds up because of the long marination and slow simmering, and it requires a bit more work than some, I hope you will agree that the results are well worth the effort. Serve with mashed potatoes or noodles.

3 pounds thick-cut bottom round of beef, cut into 2-inch cubes

4 cups Cabernet Sauvignon or other dry red wine

3 tablespoons maple syrup

3 tablespoons red wine vinegar

1½ tablespoons extra-virgin olive oil

1 onion, thinly sliced

1 carrot, thickly sliced

2 garlic cloves, chopped

4 sprigs of parsley

1 bay leaf

1½ teaspoons marjoram

1½ teaspoons salt

1 teaspoon freshly ground pepper

½ pound lean thick-sliced bacon, cut into ⅜-inch strips

1 to 2 tablespoons olive oil

1¼ pounds large pearl or small white boiling onions (about 1 inch in diameter), peeled (see Note, page 15)

¼ cup plus 2 tablespoons flour

1½ tablespoons tomato paste

½ pound peeled baby carrots or small carrots, cut in thirds

2 tablespoons chopped parsley

1. Trim any excess fat from the meat. Place in a large bowl and add 3 cups of the wine, the maple syrup, vinegar, extra-virgin olive oil, onion, carrot, garlic, parsley, bay leaf, 1 teaspoon of the marjoram, and ½ teaspoon each salt and freshly ground pepper. Cover and marinate in the refrigerator 24 to 48 hours, stirring several times.

2. Drain the marinade over a bowl to catch the liquid. Remove the cubes of beef to paper towels and pat dry. Discard the carrot; reserve the onion and parsley and bay leaf separately.

3. In a large flameproof casserole, cook the bacon in 1 tablespoon of the olive oil over moderate heat until it gives up most of its fat and begins to turn golden, about 5 minutes. Drain the bacon on paper towels.

4. Add the pearl onions to the fat remaining in the pan and cook over moderate to moderately high heat, turning them and shaking the pan, until they are nicely browned, 6 to 8 minutes. Remove and set aside.

5. Mix ¼ cup of the flour with the remaining 1 teaspoon salt and ½ teaspoon pepper. Dredge the meat in the flour, shake off any excess, and add to the casserole in 2 batches, adding the remaining oil if necessary. Cook over moderately high heat, turning, until browned. As the meat browns, remove it to a plate.

6. Add the reserved sliced onion to the pan and cook, stirring, until soft, about 5 minutes. Add the remaining 2 tablespoons flour to the pan and cook, stirring, 1 minute. Pour the reserved marinade into the casserole and bring to a boil. Stir in the tomato paste and the remaining 1 cup wine. Add the parsley, bay leaf, and remaining ½ teaspoon marjoram. Return the meat to the pan, cover, and simmer over low heat for 2 hours.

7. Add the baby carrots and simmer 20 minutes. Add the onions and bacon and simmer 10 minutes longer, or until the carrots and onions are tender and the meat is very tender. If the sauce is too thick, thin with ¼ to ⅓ cup water. Remove and discard the bay leaf. Season with additional salt and pepper to taste. Serve garnished with the chopped parsley.

➤ This stew reheats well for up to 3 days. Stored in a tightly closed container, it will freeze well for up to 6 months, but the carrots may become a bit mealy.

Carbonnade Flamande

4 to 6 Servings

H*ere's an heirloom version of the classic Belgian stew from the mother of my friend, the writer Maximilian Schlaks. The only hard part is finding the appropriate beer: dark but neither too bitter nor too sweet.*

2 pounds bottom round of beef, cut into 1-inch cubes

⅓ cup flour

1 teaspoon salt

½ teaspoon freshly ground pepper

6 tablespoons olive or peanut oil

2 pounds onions, thinly sliced (6 or 7 medium)

1 imported bay leaf

1 whole clove

2¼ cups brown Belgian beer, or Samuel Adams dark

2 or 3 medium carrots, peeled and sliced (optional)

2½ tablespoons prune butter (lekvar)

1. Toss the beef in the flour mixed with the salt and pepper. In a large flameproof casserole, heat 2½ tablespoons of the oil over moderately high heat. Add half the beef and cook, turning, until nicely browned, 8 to 10 minutes. Remove to a plate. Add another 1½ tablespoons of oil to the pan and brown the remaining beef. Reduce the heat slightly if the drippings begin to burn.

2. Add the remaining 2 tablespoons of oil to the casserole and stir in the onions. Cook, stirring occasionally, until soft, about 10 minutes.

3. Return the meat to the pan along with any juices that have collected on the plate. Toss the beef with the onions to mix. Add the bay leaf, clove, and beer. Cover, reduce the heat to low, and simmer 1½ hours, or until the meat is very tender. If you'd like the color and extra sweetness of the carrots, add them after 1 hour.

4. Remove and discard the bay leaf. Stir in the prune butter and season with additional salt and pepper to taste.

➤ This stew reheats beautifully. Stored in a tightly covered container. it will freeze well for up to 6 months.

Spicy Party Chili with Scotch Bonnet Peppers and Tequila

12 to 16 Servings

With its interesting texture from the combination of ground and cut-up meats, its fiery heat, and the added pop from the tequila, this is a chili that will liven up any party. To stretch the stew even further, serve it over rice, and don't forget the garnishes on the side: chopped sweet onion or scallions, shredded Cheddar cheese, pickled jalapeños, sour cream, and tortilla chips.

> *2 pounds boneless pork shoulder*
>
> *3 medium onions, chopped*
>
> *¼ cup vegetable oil*
>
> *4 garlic cloves, finely chopped*
>
> *2 Scotch bonnet peppers, seeded and finely minced*
>
> *1½ tablespoons cumin seeds*
>
> *⅔ cup pure mild chili powder*
>
> *3 pounds coarsely ground beef*
>
> *2 teaspoons dried oregano, preferably Mexican*
>
> *1½ teaspoons salt*
>
> *1 (28-ounce) can crushed tomatoes in heavy juice*
>
> *4 cups Simple Meat Stock (page 234) or beef stock*
>
> *½ teaspoon cayenne*
>
> *1 bay leaf*
>
> *2 cans (15 ounces each) pinto beans, rinsed and drained*
>
> *⅔ cup tequila*

1. Trim any external fat from the pork and cut the meat into roughly ⅜-inch dice.

2. In a large pot, cook the onions in the oil over moderate heat, covered, for 3 minutes. Uncover and continue to cook, stirring occasionally, until the onions are golden, about 5 minutes longer. Add the garlic, Scotch bonnet peppers, and cumin seeds and cook, stirring often, until the seeds are lightly browned and toasted, about 2 minutes. Add the chili powder and cook, stirring constantly, for 1 minute.

3. Add the ground beef, diced pork, oregano, and salt. Cook, stirring often, until the meats are no longer pink, 8 to 10 minutes. Add the crushed tomatoes, stock, cayenne, and bay leaf. Bring to a boil, reduce the heat to moderately low, and simmer, partially covered, 1½ hours. Remove and discard the bay leaf.

4. Add the beans, crushing some of them against the side of the pot with a large spoon to help thicken the sauce. Add the tequila and season with additional salt and cayenne to taste. Simmer, uncovered, for 10 minutes.

➤ As with most chilies, this tastes even better reheated and freezes well for up to 3 months, though it may need an extra dash of cayenne before serving.

Indonesian Sweet-Hot Beef with Green Beans and Carrots

6 to 8 Servings *This stew is even better reheated the next day, but don't add the green beans until just before serving, or they will lose their bright green color. Accompany with plenty of rice.*

2 tablespoons vegetable oil

2 pounds bottom round of beef, cut into 1½-inch cubes

2 medium onions, sliced

3 garlic cloves, thinly sliced

1 tablespoon minced fresh ginger

½ teaspoon crushed hot red pepper

1 salam leaf (see Note)

1 slice of dried laos root (see Note)

½ cup Ketjap Manis (recipe follows)

2 tablespoons cider vinegar

¾ pound green beans

3 medium carrots

1 teaspoon cornstarch dissolved in 1 tablespoon water

1. In a large flameproof casserole, heat the oil over moderately high heat. Add the beef in 2 batches and cook, stirring occasionally, until lightly browned, 5 to 7 minutes per batch. As the beef is done, remove it to a plate.

2. Add the onions to the casserole and cook, stirring often, until softened and just beginning to color, about 5 minutes. Add the garlic, ginger, and hot pepper and cook 1 minute longer.

3. Return the beef to the pan, along with any juices that have collected on the plate. Add 4 cups water, the salam leaf, laos root, ketjap manis, and vinegar. Bring to a boil, reduce the heat to moderately low, cover, and cook, stirring occasionally, 1½ to 1¾ hours, or until the beef is tender.

4. Meanwhile, trim the green beans and cut them diagonally into 1- to 1½ -inch pieces. In a large pot of boiling salted water, cook the green beans until they are tender, 5 to 7 minutes. Drain and rinse under cold running water;

drain well. Peel the carrots and roll-cut them by cutting down diagonally, then rotating the carrot a quarter turn and cutting diagonally again, to form triangular pieces 1 to 1½ inches long.

5. When the beef is tender, add the carrots and simmer until they are tender, 20 to 30 minutes. Stir in the dissolved cornstarch and simmer, stirring, until slightly thickened, about 2 minutes. Add the green beans just before serving and just heat through, 1 to 2 minutes.

◇ **Note:** Salam leaf and dried laos root are available at Asian markets.

➤ As mentioned in the headnote, this dish reheats beautifully. Stored in a tightly covered container, it will freeze acceptably for up to 6 months, but although the flavor will be good, the carrots will lose their texture and the green beans their texture and color.

Ketjap Manis

Makes about 3½ cups

Y*ou can buy ketjap manis in Southeast Asian groceries, but homemade is infinitely superior. It keeps for a year or longer in a bottle in the refrigerator. I learned this recipe from Copeland Marks, who has written two excellent books on Indonesian cooking.*

2½ cups sugar
1 cup water
1 (21-ounce) bottle Chinese thin soy sauce
2 salam leaves
2 pieces of dried laos root
3 garlic cloves, peeled and bruised

1. In a large flameproof casserole, stir together the sugar and water. Bring to a boil over moderately low heat and continue to boil until the syrup turns amber, about 10 minutes.

2. Immediately pour in the soy sauce. Bring to a simmer, stirring to dissolve any crystallized caramel. Add the salam leaves, laos root, and garlic. Simmer, uncovered, over low heat 15 minutes.

3. Transfer to a heatproof jar and let cool. Then cover and refrigerate. The ketjap manis will keep well in the refrigerator for at least 6 months.

Korean Braised Short Ribs

6 Servings

*C*opeland Marks, who has documented *the cooking of many exotic cuisines and recently published* The Korean Kitchen, *gave me this recipe when I reminisced about the great short ribs my friend Young Kee Kim made when we were both at the University of Chicago. Ask your butcher to cut each rib in half so they are roughly 2 inches long. Serve with plenty of white rice and steamed broccoli or brussels sprouts if you want something green.*

4 to 5 pounds short ribs of beef, cut crosswise in half

¼ cup soy sauce

6 garlic cloves, crushed through a press

1 tablespoon grated fresh ginger

2 teaspoons Asian sesame oil

1 teaspoon crushed hot red pepper

2 tablespoons olive or other vegetable oil

3 tablespoons dark brown sugar

4 scallions, thinly sliced (keep the white and green separate)

1¼ pounds small white onions (1 inch in diameter), peeled (see Note, *page 15), or 4 small yellow onions, peeled and quartered through the root*

3 medium carrots, thickly sliced on the diagonal

1. Trim excess fat from the ribs. In a large bowl, blend the soy sauce, garlic, ginger, sesame oil, and hot pepper. Add the ribs and turn to coat. Marinate for 2 to 3 hours at room temperature or overnight in the refrigerator.

2. Remove the ribs from their marinade. Scrape the seasonings clinging to the meat back into the bowl and reserve the marinade. Pat the ribs dry.

3. In a large flameproof casserole, heat the oil over moderate heat. Add the ribs in several batches and cook, turning, until lightly browned, about 5 minutes per batch. Return all the ribs to the pan. Add the marinade, brown sugar, white of scallion, and 4 cups of water. Bring to a boil, reduce the heat, cover, and simmer 45 minutes.

4. Add the onions and carrots and simmer, covered, 35 to 45 minutes, until the ribs and vegetables are tender. With a skimmer or slotted spoon, remove the ribs and vegetables to a serving dish. Skim the fat off the surface of the sauce in the pan. Pour the sauce over the meat and vegetables and serve, garnished with the scallion greens.

➤ This dish is even better made ahead, several hours or several days. Stored in a tightly covered container, the stew will freeze well for up to 6 months, though the carrots can become mealy.

Beef, Veal, and Venison Stews

Company Sukiyaki with Portobello and Shiitake Mushrooms

4 Servings

I*f you have no time to cook, here is the stew for you. All the ingredients are put out raw and cooked either right in front of the guests or on the stove in little more than 5 minutes before serving. I've chosen a combination of traditional and unusual foods, which all look pretty on the platter and taste delicious on the plate. Feel free to add or omit to your own taste and according to what you find in your market. Bean curd or bean sprouts would also be nice.*

The sauce is salty, so be sure to serve plenty of rice. If you have an Asian market near you, try jasmine rice; it has a very pleasing, distinctive flavor.

1 pound fillet of beef, sliced paper thin

1 pound fresh spinach, stemmed

2 large bunches of arugula, tough stems removed

1 large Vidalia or other sweet onion, sliced into rounds

½ pound portobello mushrooms, thickly sliced

½ pound fresh shiitake mushrooms, stems removed

1 to 2 ounces bean thread noodles

1½ tablespoons unsalted butter

1½ tablespoons sugar

¾ cup Simple Meat Stock (page 234) or reduced-sodium
    canned broth

⅓ cup sake

2 tablespoons soy sauce, preferably 1 light and 1 dark

1½ tablespoons light mirin

1 tablespoon fresh lime juice

1 tablespoon grated fresh ginger

1. On a large platter, arrange the beef, spinach, arugula, onion, portobello mushrooms, shiitake mushroom caps, and bean sprouts. If you don't plan to cook within 30 minutes, cover tightly with plastic wrap and refrigerate for up to 2 hours.

2. In a medium bowl, soak the bean thread noodles in cold water to cover until they soften, 10 to 15 minutes. Drain and rinse briefly under cold running water. With kitchen scissors, cut the noodles in half.

3. In a large heavy skillet, preferably well-seasoned cast-iron, or in a chafing dish, melt the butter over moderate heat. Sprinkle on the sugar and cook for 1 to 2 minutes until it bubbles up and begins to caramelize. Immediately pour in the stock, sake, soy sauce, mirin, and lime juice. Add the ginger and stir to mix well.

4. In batches if necessary, add the onion rounds and both types of mushrooms to the pan; they will take the longest to cook, 3 to 5 minutes. Arrange the arugula and spinach on top and cook just until wilted, 2 to 3 minutes. Add the beef slices, pushing them down into the broth if necessary, and cook briefly to desired doneness, 1 to 2 minutes; they are very thin and fillet is best rare, so watch carefully. Lastly, dip the bean thread noodles in the sauce to heat through. Immediately, remove with chopsticks or tongs and serve either on plates or over rice in bowls.

➤ This stew is made to be eaten as soon as it is cooked.

Corned Beef and Cabbage

8 to 10 Servings

T*here's nothing humble about this dish, especially when the corned beef is mated with a gorgeous bouquet of vegetables and a selection of piquant sauces. After passing heaping platters of all this delicious food, I like to offer hearty eaters a bowl of broth with which to finish up the meal. Store any leftovers in the remaining broth. Next day, remove the meat and vegetables, poach a skinned and cut-up chicken in the broth, and reheat everything together. The chicken will taste a lot like corned beef, but you'll have a second nice homey boiled dinner.*

1 (4-pound) corned beef
1 teaspoon black peppercorns
½ teaspoon allspice berries
½ teaspoon coriander seeds
3 garlic cloves, smashed
1 bay leaf
6 parsley stems
1 medium onion, stuck with 1 whole clove
3 large parsnips, peeled and quartered
3 large leeks (white and tender green), trimmed, quartered
  lengthwise, and tied into bundles
1 pound baby carrots, trimmed
¾ pound baby red potatoes, scrubbed
¾ pound baby white potatoes, scrubbed
1 pound small turnips, peeled and halved
1 medium cabbage, cut through root into 1-inch wedges
Sprigs of parsley or ¼ cup chopped parsley
Herbed Mustard Sauce (recipe follows)
Creamy Horseradish Sauce (page 87)

1. Rinse the brisket well under cold running water to remove surface brine. Place in a large stockpot and add enough cold water to cover by at least 2 inches. Bring to a boil, skimming off the foam as it rises to the surface. Immediately reduce the heat to a simmer.

2. Either tie the peppercorns, allspice, coriander, garlic, and bay leaf in a piece of cheesecloth or enclose in a tea ball; add to the pot. Tie the parsley together and add to pot along with onion stuck with clove. Cook for 1 hour, skimming frequently. When the foam stops rising, cover the pot, reduce the heat further so it doesn't go above a simmer, and cook the corned beef 3½ hours, or until fork tender.

3. Add the parsnips and leeks; simmer 10 minutes. Add the carrots and potatoes and cook 5 minutes. Add the turnips and cabbage and cook 15 to 20 minutes, or until all the vegetables are tender.

4. Carve the corned beef across the grain into thin slices. Arrange on 1 or 2 large platters and garnish with parsley. Surround the meat with the vegetables and serve hot, with a small pitcher of the broth and one or both of the suggested sauces as accompaniment.

➤ This dish is delicious reheated, as suggested in the headnote, but I never freeze it, because the texture of the vegetables will not be appealing.

Herbed Mustard Sauce

Makes about 1 cup

> ¾ *cup sour cream*
>
> *3 tablespoons Dijon mustard, preferably imported*
>
> *1½ tablespoons fresh lemon juice*
>
> ½ *teaspoon sugar*
>
> *1½ tablespoons minced fresh chives*
>
> *1½ tablespoons minced fresh dill*

In a small bowl, whisk together the sour cream, mustard, lemon juice, and sugar. Stir in the chives and dill. Cover and refrigerate for at least 1 to 2 hours before serving to allow the flavors to blend.

Creamy Horseradish Sauce

Makes about 1¾ cups

> 2½ *tablespoons unsalted butter*
>
> 2 *tablespoons flour*
>
> 1 *cup cooking broth from Corned Beef and Cabbage (page 84)*
>
> ½ *cup heavy cream*
>
> ¼ *cup freshly grated or prepared hot white horseradish*
>
> 1 *teaspoon lemon juice*
>
> ½ *teaspoon coarsely ground pepper*
>
> ¼ *teaspoon salt, or more to taste*

1. In a heavy medium saucepan, melt the butter over moderate heat. Add the flour and cook, stirring, for 1 to 2 minute without allowing the flour to color.

2. Whisk in the broth. Bring to a boil, stirring until thickened and smooth. Stir in the cream, horseradish, lemon juice, pepper, and salt. Serve hot.

Mediterranean Beef Stew
with Olives, Sun-Dried Tomatoes,
and Fresh Basil

6 to 8 Servings   *This is an exceptionally tasty stew that is good over noodles, polenta, or mashed potatoes. It can be made ahead and freezes well. Make sure to stir in the fresh basil just before serving.*

2 pounds lean beef stew meat, such as bottom round, cut into 1½-inch cubes

2 tablespoons olive oil

2 medium onions, sliced

3 garlic cloves, thinly sliced

¾ cup dry vermouth

1 (28-ounce) can Italian peeled tomatoes, coarsely chopped, juices reserved

2 teaspoons balsamic vinegar

¼ teaspoon freshly ground black pepper

⅛ teaspoon crushed hot red pepper

⅓ cup quartered and pitted Kalamata olives

⅓ cup sun-dried tomato strips packed in oil, drained

½ cup lightly packed fresh basil leaves, shredded

1. Pat the meat dry. In a large flameproof casserole, heat the olive oil over moderately high heat. Add the meat in 2 batches and cook, turning, until nicely browned, about 5 minutes per batch. As the meat is cooked, remove it to a plate.

2. Add the onions and cook, stirring occasionally, until they are golden and beginning to brown around the edges, about 5 minutes. Add the garlic and cook until softened and fragrant, about 1 minute. Pour in the vermouth and boil until reduced by half, 1 to 2 minutes. Then add the chopped tomatoes with their juices, the vinegar, black pepper, hot pepper, and 1½ cups water.

3. Add the meat to the sauce, along with any juices that have collected on the plate. Bring to a boil, reduce the heat to low, cover, and simmer 1¼ hours. Add the olives and simmer 20 to 30 minutes longer, or until the meat is tender.

4. Add the sun-dried tomatoes and simmer 5 minutes. (The stew can be made to this point up to 2 days in advance.) Just before serving, stir in the fresh basil.

➤ Stored in a tightly covered container, this stew will freeze well for up to 6 months, though the basil will darken in color. You might want to freshen it up with some fresh shredded basil or chopped parsley.

Cuban Picadillo

4 to 6 Servings $\quad$ T*his is an old family recipe that I have made for many years. Even though it is based on ground meat, the olives, almonds, capers, and raisins dress it up enough for company. Serve with steamed white rice and Braised Black Beans (recipe follows). Fried plantains are also a lovely accompaniment.*

1½ pounds lean ground beef
1½ teaspoons salt
½ teaspoon freshly ground pepper
1½ teaspoons dried oregano
1½ cups dry sherry, preferably amontillado
3 tablespoons fruity olive oil
2 medium onions, chopped
1 small green bell pepper, chopped
3 garlic cloves, chopped
1½ teaspoons ground cumin
1 (6-ounce) can tomato paste
2 tablespoons tiny (nonpareil) capers with their brine
1 imported bay leaf
½ cup raisins
½ cup slivered blanched almonds
½ cup sliced Spanish olives

1. In a medium bowl, combine the meat with 1 teaspoon salt, ¼ teaspoon pepper, ½ teaspoon oregano, and ¾ cup of the sherry. Mix with your hands to blend well and set aside at room temperature for 30 to 60 minutes.

2. In a large skillet or flameproof casserole, heat the olive oil over moderately high heat. Add the onions and sauté for 2 minutes. Add the bell pepper and garlic and cook, stirring often, until the onion is just beginning to brown, about 5 minutes longer. Add the cumin and cook for 30 seconds. Add the meat and cook, stirring to break up large lumps, until the meat is no longer pink, 5 to 7 minutes. Add the tomato paste, capers with their brine, bay leaf, remaining salt, pepper, oregano, and sherry, and 1 cup of water. Bring to a boil, stirring to

mix well. Reduce the heat to moderately low, cover, and simmer 15 minutes.

3. Gently stir in the raisins, almonds, and olives. If the stew seems too thick, add another ½ cup water. Cover and simmer 15 minutes longer. Season with additional salt and pepper to taste. Remove and discard the bay leaf before serving.

➤ Picadillo tastes even better if reheated after standing for a couple of hours or even after being refrigerated for a day or two. Stored in a tightly covered container, it will freeze well for up to 3 months.

Braised Black Beans

Y*ou will get much better results here
and the beans will be more digestible if you soak them overnight. Be sure
to rinse them well before you soak them because, to maintain their inky black
color, I cook them right in their soaking water.*

> 1 pound dried black beans
> 1 large onion, preferably white, finely chopped
> 1 small green bell pepper, chopped
> 3 garlic cloves, chopped
> 1½ teaspoons dried oregano
> 1 teaspoon ground cumin
> 1 bay leaf
> 1½ tablespoons red wine vinegar or sherry wine vinegar
> Salt
> Freshly ground black pepper

1. Place the beans in a colander and rinse well under cold running water. Pick over to remove any stones or grit and place the beans in a large pot. Add enough water to cover by at least 2 inches. Let soak overnight.

2. Bring the beans and their soaking liquid to a boil, skimming off any foam that rises to the top. Add the onion, bell pepper, garlic, oregano, cumin, and bay leaf. Simmer 1½ hours, or until the beans are very tender and beginning to fall apart. The mixture should be soupy; if it becomes too dry, add a little more water.

3. Remove about 2 cups of the beans with their liquid and puree them through the medium blade of a food mill or in a food processor. Return to the pot. Stir in the wine vinegar and season the beans with salt and pepper to taste. Remove the bay leaf before serving.

Ropa Vieja

6 Servings

As a bit of food trivia, you might like to know that ropa vieja *literally means "old clothes," a reference to the tattered appearance of the meat, which is torn apart in large shreds. This savory Cuban dish is really more of a braised meat, but I've turned it into a stew and made it more contemporary by increasing the proportion of vegetable and sauce to meat. Serve with white rice, Braised Black Beans (see page 92), and fried plantains.*

1¾ pounds skirt steak or flank steak

2 medium yellow onions, chopped

1 medium carrot, chopped

8 garlic cloves, chopped

1 bay leaf

1 teaspoon dried oregano

1 teaspoon salt

½ teaspoon freshly ground pepper

1 tablespoon sherry wine vinegar

¼ cup extra-virgin olive oil

2 large green bell peppers, cut into long, thin strips

1 medium red bell pepper, cut into long, thin strips

1 large white onion, sliced ¼ inch thick

¼ teaspoon ground annatto or a small pinch of saffron

1½ cups tomato puree

1. Trim off any excess fat from the meat and cut the steak lengthwise in half. Cut each half crosswise into 3 pieces each. Place the meat in a large flame-proof casserole and add 6 cups of water. Bring to a boil, skimming off all the grayish scum that rises to the top.

2. Add 1 of the chopped yellow onions, the carrot, half the garlic, the bay leaf, oregano, salt, pepper, and vinegar. Bring to a boil, reduce the heat to moderately low, cover, and cook for 1¾ to 2 hours, or until the meat is falling apart.

3. Remove the meat and tear into long shreds, using 2 forks or your fingers. Strain the cooking liquid and reserve 2½ cups of the broth. (If there is more than 3½ cups, boil to reduce so the flavor is strong enough.)

4. In a large flameproof casserole, heat 2 tablespoons of the olive oil. Add the bell peppers and white onion and sauté over moderately high heat, stirring often, until crisp-tender, about 5 minutes. With a slotted spoon, remove the vegetables to a bowl.

5. Add the remaining 2 tablespoons oil and the second chopped yellow onion to the oil remaining in the pan, reduce the heat to moderate, and cook, stirring occasionally, until softened and beginning to turn golden, 3 to 5 minutes. Add the remaining garlic and cook 1 minute longer. Stir in the annatto. Add the tomato puree and reserved meat broth and simmer, uncovered, for 10 minutes.

6. Season the sauce with additional salt and pepper to taste. Add the shredded meat and sautéed peppers and onion, reduce the heat to moderately low, and simmer, partially covered, 5 minutes.

➤ This stew reheats well. Stored in a tightly covered container, it can be frozen for up to 6 months, though the peppers and onions will lose some of their texture.

Spezzatino of Veal with Fennel

4 to 6 Servings   I *thank Teresa Harsymczuk, a great Roman cook, for the following two veal stews. Even the small amounts of pancetta (Italian unsmoked bacon) called for add a lovely richness and body to the sauce. Serve this ragout with risotto or pasta and steamed broccoli or sautéed escarole.*

3 tablespoons olive oil

3 tablespoons finely diced pancetta

2 onions, chopped

1 celery rib, chopped

3 garlic cloves, chopped

2½ pounds veal stew meat

½ teaspoon salt

¼ teaspoon freshly ground pepper

1½ tablespoons tomato paste

1 cup dry red wine

1 tablespoon flour

2 cups Simple Meat Stock (page 234) or water

¼ cup coarsely chopped parsley

½ teaspoon fennel seeds

1. In a large flameproof casserole, heat the oil over moderate heat. Add the pancetta, onions, and celery. Cook until the pancetta is lightly browned, 3 to 5 minutes. Add 2 of the chopped garlic cloves and cook 2 minutes longer.

2. Add the veal to the pan and toss to coat with the oil. Season with the salt and pepper. Add the tomato paste and the wine. Bring to a boil, reduce the heat to a simmer, and cook, uncovered, until the wine evaporates, 20 to 30 minutes.

3. Sprinkle the flour over the veal and toss to mix in. Pour in enough stock or water to cover. Return to a boil, reduce the heat to low, cover, and simmer until the sauce thickens and the meat is tender, about 1 hour.

4. Just before serving, chop together the remaining garlic with the parsley and fennel seeds. Stir into the stew. Simmer 5 minutes.

➤ Stored in a tightly closed container, this stew will keep well in the refrigerator for up to 3 days or in the freezer for up to 6 months.

Stufatino alla Romana

4 to 6 Servings

This Roman dish is attractive served within a Parmesan Polenta Ring (recipe follows), perhaps with a bouquet of sautéed mushrooms, baby onions, and zucchini on the side.

> 2 tablespoons olive oil
> 3 tablespoons finely diced pancetta
> 2 medium onions, chopped
> 2 garlic cloves, chopped
> 2½ pounds veal stew meat, cut into 1-inch pieces
> ¾ teaspoon marjoram
> ½ teaspoon salt
> ¼ teaspoon freshly ground pepper
> 1 cup dry red wine
> 1½ pounds plum tomatoes, peeled, seeded, and chopped, or
>   1 (28-ounce) can Italian peeled tomatoes, drained
>   and chopped
> 1½ to 2 cups Simple Meat Stock (page 234) or water

1. In a large flameproof casserole, heat the oil over moderate heat. Add the pancetta, onions, and garlic and cook, stirring occasionally, until the onions are softened and the pancetta is lightly browned, 5 to 7 minutes.

2. Add the veal and season with the marjoram, salt, and pepper. Toss the meat over moderately high heat to brown lightly. Add the wine and simmer, uncovered, until the wine is evaporated to a tablespoon or two, about 20 minutes.

3. Add the tomatoes and simmer, uncovered, until they begin to turn to sauce, about 5 minutes. Pour in 1½ cups of the stock, or enough to just cover the meat; partially cover the pan, and simmer over low heat until the veal is tender and the sauce has thickened, about 1 hour. Season with additional salt and pepper to taste before serving.

➤ Stored in a tightly closed container, this stew will keep well in the refrigerator for up to 3 days or in the freezer for up to 6 months.

Parmesan Polenta Ring

4 to 6 Servings

While I prefer stews and their accompaniments served family style, in large bowls and serving dishes, you can mold this polenta into individual timbales and unmold onto separate plates if you prefer. If you make the polenta ring ahead of time, reheat it in a microwave or in the oven.

1½ teaspoons salt
⅛ teaspoon cayenne
1½ cups instant polenta
3 tablespoons unsalted butter
¾ cup freshly grated imported Parmesan cheese

1. Line a 4- to 6-cup ring mold with plastic wrap, letting the excess overhang the edges. Smooth the plastic wrap neatly into the pan so that the unmolded polenta will look attractive.

2. In a large saucepan, bring 6 cups of water, salt, and cayenne to a boil. Gradually stir in the polenta and cook over moderately low heat, stirring, until the mixture is thickened and begins to pull away in a mass, about 5 minutes.

3. Stir in the butter until melted. Mix in the cheese. Turn the polenta into the ring mold, packing it in tightly. Let stand 5 to 10 minutes, until set; then invert to unmold and peel off the plastic wrap.

Osso Buco

Braised veal shanks are one of the silkiest of meats; and with the creamy marrow in the center of the bone, those of us who love them enjoy the texture almost as much as the flavor. My version of this classic Italian preparation adds extra carrots and white wine and just a little mushroom for added depth of flavor. Serve with a simple risotto flavored with Parmesan cheese or with the slightly bitter version, with grilled radicchio and endive, that follows.

4 pounds veal shanks, cut into 1½-inch lengths

¼ cup flour

1 teaspoon salt

½ teaspoon freshly ground pepper

¼ cup olive oil

1½ cups dry white wine

2 tablespoons butter

1 medium onion, chopped

1 medium leek (white and tender green), well rinsed
    and chopped

1 large celery rib with leaves, chopped

4 medium carrots, 1 chopped and 3 roll-cut into ¾-inch lengths
    (see page 77, Step 4)

4 medium mushrooms, chopped

5 garlic cloves, minced

½ pound tomatoes, peeled, seeded, and chopped

3 cups Simple Meat Stock (page 234) or Rich Chicken Stock
    (page 232)

1 bay leaf

¾ teaspoon dried thyme leaves

⅓ cup chopped Italian parsley

Zest from 1 lemon

1. Trim any excess fat from the veal shanks, leaving intact all the skin and membrane that holds the meat together. Place the flour in a shallow bowl and mix with the salt and pepper. Dredge the veal shanks in the seasoned flour to coat. Reserve any flour remaining in the bowl.

2. In a large skillet, heat 3 tablespoons of the olive oil over moderately high heat. Add the veal shanks in batches without crowding and sauté, turning, until nicely browned all over, about 8 minutes per batch. As the veal is browned, remove to a plate. Reduce the heat if the flour on the bottom begins to burn. Pour out any fat in the pan. Add the wine and bring to a boil, scraping up all the browned bits from the bottom of the pan. Boil until the wine is reduced to about 1 cup, about 3 minutes. Remove from the heat.

3. In a large flameproof casserole, melt the butter in the remaining 1 tablespoon oil. Add the onion and leek and cook over moderate heat, stirring occasionally, until the onion is golden, 5 to 7 minutes. Add the celery, chopped carrot, mushrooms, and 2 of the minced garlic cloves. Cook, stirring occasionally, until the celery and carrot are softened, 5 to 7 minutes longer. Sprinkle the reserved seasoned flour over the vegetables in the casserole and cook, stirring, for 1 minute.

4. Pour the reduced wine into the pan. Bring to a boil, stirring until smooth. Add the tomatoes, stock, bay leaf, thyme, and 2 tablespoons of the chopped parsley. Return the veal shanks to the casserole. Bring to a boil, reduce the heat, cover, and simmer over low heat 1 hour. Add the cut carrots and continue to simmer, covered, 30 minutes longer, or until the veal is meltingly tender. Remove the veal shanks and carrots to a large serving dish.

5. Chop together the remaining parsley and minced garlic with the lemon zest. Stir into the sauce, season with additional salt and pepper to taste, pour over the veal shanks, and serve.

➤ Stored in a tightly covered container, this stew keeps well in the refrigerator for up to 3 days and in the freezer for up to 3 months.

Risotto with Grilled Radicchio and Endive

6 Servings

I*f you like a hint of bitterness, you'll particularly enjoy this rice. Both the radicchio and endive are made nuttier in flavor by grilling them — either over a barbecue or on a grill pan — before they are shredded and added to the rice. This dish goes nicely with both the Osso Buco on page 98 and the Spezzatino of Veal with Fennel on page 95. It would also make a perfectly respectable first course.*

1 small head of radicchio

1 large Belgian endive

2 tablespoons olive oil

4 tablespoons unsalted butter

3 shallots, minced

1½ cups Arborio rice

¼ cup Madeira

4½ to 5 cups Rich Chicken Stock (page 232) or Vegetable Stock
   (page 235) or 2 cans (14½ ounces each) reduced-sodium
   chicken broth or vegetable broth mixed with enough water
   to equal 4 cups

½ cup grated Parmesan cheese

Salt

Freshly ground black pepper

1. Light a medium-hot fire in a barbecue grill or preheat a cast-iron grill pan on top of the stove. Cut the radicchio and endive in half lengthwise and brush all over with some of the olive oil. Grill, turning, until lightly browned all over, about 8 minutes. Cut the grilled radicchio and endive crosswise into thin shreds. Set aside.

2. In a large saucepan, melt 2 tablespoons of the butter in the remaining oil. Add the shallots and cook over moderate heat until softened, about 2 minutes. Add the rice and cook, stirring, until the grains are coated with oil and turn slightly opaque, about 3 minutes. Add the Madeira and cook, stirring, until most

of the liquid evaporates, 1 to 2 minutes. Add 1 cup of the stock and cook, stirring with a wooden spoon, until most of it is absorbed. Add another ½ cup and continue to cook until almost absorbed. Continue this process until the rice is tender with a slight bite remaining in the center and the sauce is thick and soupy, a total of 25 to 30 minutes.

3. Immediately stir in the remaining 2 tablespoons butter until melted. Stir in the shredded radicchio and endive and then the Parmesan cheese. Season lightly with salt and generously with pepper to taste. Serve at once.

Lemony Blanquette of Veal with Asparagus and Mushrooms

4 to 6 Servings

A *blanquette is a white stew, where the meat is gently poached rather than browned first and the sauce is finished with egg yolks and cream. Light, elegant, and just creamy enough to feel luxurious, this stew is a classic for good reason. Serve with rice or with boiled new potatoes.*

2 pounds veal stew meat, such as shoulder, cut into
    1- to 1½-inch cubes

2 onions, coarsely chopped

2 leeks (white part only), well rinsed and coarsely chopped

2 carrots, peeled and coarsely chopped

2 celery ribs, chopped

1 medium turnip, peeled and chopped

3 garlic cloves, chopped

1½ cups dry white wine

6 parsley stems

1 bay leaf

Grated zest and juice from 1 lemon

1 pound fresh asparagus

2 tablespoons unsalted butter, softened

2 tablespoons flour

12 ounces mushrooms, quartered

2 egg yolks

⅔ cup heavy cream

Dash of cayenne

Salt

1. Rinse the veal very well. Place it in a large flameproof casserole and add 6 cups of cold water. Bring to a boil, skimming off all the foam that rises to the top. Add the chopped onions, leeks, carrots, celery, turnip, garlic, white wine, parsley, bay leaf, lemon zest, and lemon juice. Return the liquid to a bare simmer, partially cover the pot, and cook over low heat 1¼ to 1½ hours, or until the veal is meltingly tender.

2. Meanwhile, cut the tough stems off the asparagus and cut the asparagus crosswise on the diagonal into 1½-inch pieces. In a large saucepan of boiling salted water, cook the asparagus until just tender, 2 to 3 minutes. Drain, rinse under cold running water, and drain well. Set aside.

3. Drain the veal and vegetables into a fine sieve set over a bowl. Pick out the meat and set aside. Press gently to extract as much liquid as possible from the chopped vegetables in the sieve; discard the vegetables. Rinse out the casserole and measure the reserved liquid back into the pot. There will be about 5 cups. Boil, uncovered, until reduced to 3 cups.

4. In a small bowl, mash together the butter and flour to make a smooth paste. Add the mushrooms to the stock in the casserole and cook over moderate heat for 3 minutes. Gradually stir in the butter paste and boil 2 minutes, stirring until thickened and smooth.

5. In a medium bowl, whisk the egg yolks with the cream. Gradually whisk in 1 cup of the hot sauce. Whisk the cream mixture into the sauce remaining in the pan. Return the veal to the pan and simmer over moderately low heat for 2 minutes. Season with the cayenne and salt to taste. Add the asparagus, simmer 1 minute, and serve.

➤ Much to my surprise, I found that this stew was good reheated, even after up to 2 days in the refrigerator or 6 months in the freezer. Because of the flour in the sauce, you don't have to worry about the sauce curdling when you reheat it.

Veal Shanks with Wild Mushrooms and Madeira

6 Servings

I love red wine and brown food, and this is about as brown as it comes. The veal is so unctuous that no added enrichment is needed, and the flavor is pure mushroom. Serve with a simple risotto or over buttered pasta.

½ cup dried porcini pieces (about ½ ounce)

⅓ cup flour

1 teaspoon salt

½ teaspoon freshly ground pepper

4 pounds veal shanks, cut into 1½-inch lengths

5 tablespoons olive oil

1 cup dry white wine

3 tablespoons unsalted butter

½ pound fresh mushrooms, sliced

4 large shallots, minced

½ pound fresh shiitake mushrooms, stemmed and halved

½ pound Italian brown mushrooms (cremini), quartered

½ teaspoon dried tarragon

⅔ cup Madeira

2 cups Brown Chicken Stock (page 233) or Simple Meat Stock (page 234)

Dash of cayenne

2 tablespoons minced parsley

1. Place the dried porcini in a small heatproof bowl and cover with 1 cup boiling water. Let soak 15 minutes, or until softened. Lift them out of the water and squeeze as much liquid as possible back into the bowl. Rinse any grit off, pat dry, and chop coarsely. Strain and reserve the liquid.

2. Season the flour with the salt and pepper and place in a shallow bowl. Dredge the veal shanks in the flour to coat. In a large skillet, heat 3 tablespoons of the oil. Add the veal shanks in batches without crowding and sauté over

moderately high heat, turning, until the veal is nicely browned all over, about 8 minutes per batch. Remove to a plate as the meat browns.

3. Pour off all the fat in the skillet. Add the wine and bring to a boil, scraping up the brown bits from the bottom of the pan. Boil over high heat until the wine is reduced by about one-third, 3 to 5 minutes. Remove from the heat and set aside.

4. In a large flameproof casserole, melt 1½ tablespoons of the butter in 1 tablespoon of the olive oil over moderately high heat. Add the fresh mushrooms, half the shallots, and half the shiitakes. Sauté, tossing often, until the mushroom juices evaporate and the mushrooms begin to brown, about 5 minutes. Scrape into a bowl. Melt the remaining butter in the remaining oil. Add the Italian brown mushrooms and the remaining shallots and shiitakes. Sauté, tossing until lightly browned, about 5 minutes.

5. Return the cooked mushrooms and any juices in the bowl to the pan. Add the dried porcini, tarragon, and Madeira. Boil until the Madeira is reduced by half, about 2 minutes. Add the reserved wine from the skillet, the stock, reserved mushroom liquid, and cayenne. Return the veal to the pan along with any juices that have collected on the plate. Bring to a boil, reduce the heat to low, cover, and cook 1½ hours, or until the veal is meltingly tender.

6. With a slotted spoon or skimmer, remove the veal shanks and mushrooms to a serving dish. Boil the sauce until slightly reduced and thickened, about 3 minutes. Season with additional salt and pepper to taste. Pour over the veal and serve, garnished with the parsley.

➤ This recipe reheats well for up to 2 days. Stored in a tightly closed container, it can be frozen for up to 3 months.

Venison Chili with Black Beans and Roasted Peppers

12 to 14 Servings

T*his is a mild chili, sweetly spiced and made more complex with the interesting but almost undetectable undertones of chocolate. It improves if allowed to stand before serving.*

If you have no venison, top round beef can be substituted. If you prefer your chili hot, pass a bottle of pepper sauce at the table. If you like lots of beans in your chili, this has room for a couple more cans, in which case it will serve upward of 16 to 20 people.

6 large or 8 medium ancho chile peppers

3 pounds venison

¼ pound lean bacon, chopped

3 medium onions

6 garlic cloves

3 fresh green chile peppers

1½ tablespoons ground cumin

2 teaspoons dried oregano

1½ teaspoons cinnamon

1½ pounds ground pork shoulder

2 teaspoons salt

½ teaspoon freshly grond pepper

2 cups full-bodied red wine, such as Cabernet Sauvignon

1 (28-ounce) can Italian peeled tomatoes, coarsely chopped, with their juices

2 cups Simple Meat Stock (page 234) or canned broth

1 bay leaf

1½ ounces semisweet chocolate

1½ tablespoons sherry wine vinegar

6 bell peppers, of assorted colors, roasted, peeled, seeded, and cut into ⅜-inch dice

2 cans (15 ounces each) black beans, rinsed and drained

1½ tablespoons masa harina or yellow cornmeal

1. In a large hot, dry cast-iron skillet or on a griddle, toast the ancho chile peppers lightly over moderate heat, turning with tongs, until softened, about 10 seconds per side. Transfer to a medium heatproof bowl and pour on 4 cups of boiling water. Soak 30 minutes. Drain the chiles; strain and reserve 1½ cups of the soaking water. Remove the stems, seeds, and ribs. In a blender or food processor, puree the chiles with the reserved soaking water. Cut the venison into roughly ⅜-inch dicc.

2. In a large flameproof casserole, cook the bacon over moderate heat, stirring occasionally, until it is lightly browned and has given up most of its fat, 5 to 7 minutes. Remove with a slotted spoon and set aside.

3. Preheat the oven to 325 degrees F. Add the onions to the pan, stir to coat with the fat, cover, and cook 2 minutes. Uncover, raise the heat to moderately high and cook, stirring occasionally, until golden and just beginning to brown, about 7 minutes longer. Add the garlic, ancho chile peppers, cumin, oregano, and cinnamon and cook, stirring, 1 to 2 minutes, until the garlic is softened and fragrant. Mix in the pork. Add the venison, salt, and pepper and cook, stirring often, until the meat is no longer pink, 8 to 10 minutes. Stir in the wine, chile puree, tomatoes with their juices, stock, bay leaf, and bacon. Cover and transfer to the oven. Bake 2 hours.

4. Transfer the casserole to the stovetop. Skim off as much fat from the surface of the chili as you can. Place the chocolate in a small heatproof bowl. Ladle on 1 to 1½ cups of the hot chili and stir until the chocolate is melted and blended. Stir back into the chili in the casserole. Add the wine vinegar, roasted peppers, and black beans and simmer, uncovered, over moderate heat for 15 minutes. Sprinkle the masa harina lightly over the surface of the chili as you stir it in. Simmer until slightly thickened, 5 to 10 minutes longer. If you have time, let stand at least 2 hours at room temperature or refrigerate overnight, then reheat before serving.

➤ Like most chilies, this one is even better reheated after a day or two. Stored in a tightly covered container, it will freeze well for up to 3 months.

Venison Stew with Armagnac and Prunes

Game meats in general benefit from *marinating before cooking, both to tenderize them and to add balancing flavor. Here the venison is marinated for at least a full day. Because the meat is so lean, it does very well with moist, slow braising in stews. Serve this rich sauce with polenta, mashed potatoes, or noodles.*

1½ to 2 pounds venison, cut into 1½-inch chunks

2 medium onions, sliced

2 medium carrots, sliced

2 garlic cloves, crushed through a press

5 large sprigs of parsley

1 teaspoon dried thyme leaves

2 cups dry red wine

½ cup Armagnac

2 tablespoons extra-virgin olive oil

1½ tablespoons red wine vinegar

½ teaspoon marjoram

1 bay leaf

1 teaspoon salt

½ teaspoon freshly ground pepper

3 tablespoons olive oil

2 tablespoons flour

1½ cups Simple Meat Stock (page 234) or water

1½ tablespoons tomato paste

1 (1-pound) box pitted prunes

1. Place the venison in a large stainless steel bowl. Add the onions, carrots, garlic, parsley, and thyme. Toss to mix. Pour on the wine, ¼ cup of the Armagnac, the extra-virgin olive oil, vinegar, and marjoram. Add the bay leaf, cover, and marinate in the refrigerator 24 to 48 hours.

2. Remove the venison from the marinade and pat dry. Season with the salt and pepper. Drain the marinade through a sieve over a bowl. Reserve the vegetables and the liquid separately. Discard the parsley sprigs. Set the bay leaf aside.

3. In a large flameproof casserole, heat 2 tablespoons of the olive oil over moderately high heat. Add the venison in 2 or 3 batches and sauté, turning, until browned, about 7 minutes per batch. As the meat browns, remove it to a bowl.

4. Add the remaining 1 tablespoon oil and the onions and carrots from the marinade to the casserole and cook, stirring occasionally, until all excess liquid boils away and the carrots and onions begin to brown, about 7 minutes. Sprinkle the flour over the vegetables and cook, stirring, 1 minute. Pour in the marinade liquid and bring to a boil, stirring until slightly thickened and smooth, 1 to 2 minutes.

5. Stir in the stock and tomato paste and add the bay leaf. Return the venison to the casserole along with any liquid in the bowl. Bring to a boil, cover, reduce the heat to low, and simmer until the venison is tender, about 2 hours.

6. Meanwhile, soak the prunes in the remaining ¼ cup Armagnac and 2 tablespoons hot water for at least 20 minutes. Add to the stew and simmer for 10 to 15 minutes before serving.

➤ This stew reheats beautifully, though with repeated boiling the prunes will begin to blend into the sauce. Stored in a tightly covered container, it will freeze well for up to 3 months.

Pork Stews

It's an old story how lean the new pork is, so I won't go into it. Suffice it to say that because of new breeding and feeding practices, today's hog contains roughly 31 percent less fat content (with 14 percent fewer calories) than its ancestor of only a decade ago. While this new meat is probably more healthful for you, many cooks miss the attendant loss of moisture and taste. Stews, however, with their slow, moist braising, are able to take advantage of the subtle, rich flavor of pork and still provide the nutritional benefits of its relative leanness without ending up dry or tough.

Fattier, more economical cuts of the pig, such as the shoulder, can make excellent stews, but in most cases, I have opted, as elsewhere in this book, for the leanest cut: the loin. Besides its lower fat and cholesterol count, the loin presents little work; there is only a firm layer of outer fat that's easy to trim off.

Pork stews cook on average in an hour and a half. They are almost invariably better reheated. And depending upon the vegetables included, many of them freeze exceptionally well. However, root

vegetables, such as potatoes, carrots, and turnips, turn mealy, while whole onions, peppers, and green beans lose their texture.

Pork stew can be light, as in the Rosemary Ragout of Pork with Zucchini and Sweet Peppers; but to be honest, I am most fond of its heartier versions. Recipes like Barbecued Country Ribs Stew with Sweet Potatoes and Black-Eyed Peas, which are served with a colorful topping of Sautéed Collards and Kale, a Neapolitan Ragout of Sausages and Peppers, and Pork and Sausage Goulash — all perfect one-dish meals — show off the great stewing potential of pork.

Adobo of Pork with Chayote, Carrots, and Sugar Snap Peas

6 to 8 Servings

*C*hayote is a very mild, pale green squash that is particularly nice in stews because it retains its texture. While sugar snap peas are not exactly Mexican, peas are common in Latin cooking, and I took the liberty of using these instead for their bright green color and crispy crunch. Serve this stew with plain rice or dress it up with the Mexican Risotto that follows.

7 ancho chile peppers
1 medium onion, chopped
3 garlic cloves, chopped
1 teaspoon dried oregano, preferably Mexican
1¼ teaspoons ground cumin
½ teaspoon ground cinnamon
1 teaspoon salt
2 pounds lean boneless pork, cut into 1-inch cubes
1½ tablespoons vegetable oil
2½ cups Simple Meat Stock (page 234) or water
1½ tablespoons lime juice
1 tablespoon cider vinegar
1 tablespoon dark brown sugar
4 medium carrots, peeled and cut on the bias into 1½-inch
    lengths
2 chayotes, peeled, pitted, and cut into 1-inch chunks
½ pound sugar snap peas
2 tablespoons coarsely chopped cilantro

1. Heat a dry heavy skillet or griddle, preferably cast-iron, over moderate heat. Toast the ancho chile peppers, turning, about 10 seconds per side to soften them slightly, but do not let them brown or they will taste burned. As they are toasted, place the chiles in a large heatproof bowl. When all the chiles are done, pour 2 cups boiling water over them and let soak 20 to 30 minutes, until soft.

2. Remove the chiles, reserving the soaking liquid. Tear the chiles in half and remove the stems and seeds. Place the chiles in a blender or food processor. Add half the chopped onion, the garlic, oregano, cumin, cinnamon, and salt. Strain the chile soaking water into the blender and puree until smooth. Set the chile sauce aside.

3. Trim any excess fat from the pork. In a large flameproof casserole, heat the oil over moderately high heat. Add the remaining chopped onion and the pork and sauté, stirring occasionally, until the meat is nicely browned, 15 to 20 minutes.

4. Pour the chile sauce over the meat, reduce the heat to moderate, and continue to cook, stirring often, and scraping the bottom of the pan with a wooden spoon to prevent scorching, for 5 minutes. Add the stock, lime juice, cider vinegar, and brown sugar. Bring to a boil, reduce the heat to low, cover, and simmer 30 minutes.

5. Add the carrots and chayotes and simmer 35 to 45 minutes, until the pork and vegetables are tender.

6. Meanwhile, in a medium saucepan of boiling salted water, cook the sugar snap peas until they are bright green and crisp-tender, about 2 minutes. Drain and rinse under cold running water; drain well. Add to the stew and heat through. Serve, garnished with the cilantro.

➤ This stew reheats well after a day or two in the refrigerator. Because of the vegetables used here, I do not freeze this dish.

Mexican Risotto

6 to 8 Servings

> 2 tablespoons olive oil
>
> 1 medium onion, chopped
>
> 1½ teaspoons cumin seeds
>
> 1 teaspoon dried oregano, preferably Mexican
>
> 1 or 2 minced jalapeño or serrano peppers or ¼ to ½ teaspoon
>   crushed hot red pepper, to taste
>
> 1½ cups long-grain white rice
>
> 3 cups Rich Chicken Stock (page 232) or reduced-sodium
>   canned broth
>
> 1 (7-ounce) can diced roasted green chiles, drained
>
> 1½ cups corn kernels, fresh, frozen, or canned
>
> ⅔ cup sour cream
>
> 1 cup shredded sharp Cheddar cheese
>
> ½ teaspoon salt

1. Heat the oil in a large saucepan. Add the onion and cook over moderately high heat, stirring often, until golden and just beginning to brown at the edges, 5 to 7 minutes.

2. Add the cumin seeds, oregano, and minced or crushed hot pepper(s) and cook, stirring, 1 to 2 minutes, until the cumin smells fragrant. Add the rice and cook, stirring constantly, to coat with the oil, 1 to 2 minutes longer.

3. Pour in the stock and stir once. Bring to a boil, cover, and reduce the heat to low. Cook 15 to 20 minutes, until the liquid is absorbed and the rice is tender but still firm.

4. Remove from the heat and stir in the diced chiles, corn, sour cream, cheese, and salt. Serve at once or turn the mixture into a 2- to 2½-quart casserole or baking dish. Cover and set aside for up to 2 hours or refrigerate for up to 2 days. Let return to room temperature before reheating either in a microwave oven or in a 350 degree F. oven for 20 to 25 minutes.

Barbecued Country Ribs Stew with Sweet Potatoes and Black-Eyed Peas

6 Servings   *This is a rustic Southern-inspired stew that's down-home and fun to eat. Serve with corn bread on the side.*

4 pounds lean country-style ribs, trimmed of all excess fat
¾ teaspoon salt
½ teaspoon freshly ground black pepper
2 tablespoons vegetable oil
2 medium onions, finely chopped
1½ tablespoons ground cumin
1 tablespoon paprika
½ teaspoon cayenne, or less to taste
2 cups Simple Meat Stock (page 234) or Rich Chicken Stock
    (page 232) or reduced-sodium canned broth
1 (14½-ounce) can recipe-ready diced tomatoes in juice
⅓ cup cider vinegar
1 orange, juice and grated zest (⅔ cup juice, 1 tablespoon zest)
1½ tablespoons soy sauce
1½ tablespoons brown sugar
1½ tablespoons minced fresh ginger
3 garlic cloves, crushed through a press
3 medium sweet potatoes (1½ pounds), peeled and cut into
    ½-inch-thick rounds
1 (15-ounce) can black-eyed peas, rinsed and drained
Sautéed Collards and Kale (recipe follows)

1. Preheat the oven to 350 degrees F.

2. Season the ribs with ½ teaspoon each salt and pepper. In a large stewpot, heat the oil. Add the ribs in batches and cook over moderately high heat, turning, until browned, 7 to 9 minutes per batch. Remove to a platter.

3. Pour off all but 2 tablespoons fat from the pan. Add the onions, reduce the heat to moderate, and cook, stirring, until they are golden and beginning to brown, 8 to 10 minutes. Add the cumin, paprika, and cayenne and cook, stirring, 1 minute. Pour in the stock and bring to a boil, stirring up the brown bits from the bottom of the pan. Add the tomatoes with their juice, the vinegar, orange juice and zest, soy sauce, brown sugar, ginger, garlic, and ¼ teaspoon salt.

4. Return the ribs to the casserole, cover, and transfer to the oven. Bake 1 hour. Remove the ribs to a platter and skim as much fat as possible off the sauce in the pan. Return the ribs to the pan. Add the sweet potatoes, pushing them down gently so they are underneath the liquid; if necessary, lift up several of the ribs and put them on top. Return to the oven and bake 30 minutes, or until the sweet potatoes are just tender and the ribs are almost falling apart; stir up the potatoes gently after 15 minutes to be sure they cook evenly.

5. Add the black-eyed peas and bake 5 to 10 minutes longer, until the sweet potatoes are tender and the flavors are blended. Serve in bowls, with the Sautéed Collards and Kale sprinkled on top.

➤ As with many tomato-based or barbecue-sauced dishes, this one reheats well after being refrigerated for a day or two. It has never lasted long enough for me to freeze, and that's probably for the best, because I suspect the sweet potatoes would fall apart.

Sautéed Collards and Kale

This recipe was developed by CIA graduate Amy Howarth, who was a great help in testing this book. It will look as if you have a mountain of these greens when you prepare them but, like fresh spinach, they shrink substantially when cooked.

> *1 large bunch of collards (1¼ pounds)*
> *1 large bunch of kale (1¼ pounds)*
> *3 tablespoons olive oil*
> *6 garlic cloves, finely chopped*
> *½ teaspoon salt*
> *½ teaspoon freshly ground pepper*
> *4 teaspoons fresh lemon juice*

1. Rinse the collards and kale well in a large bowl of cold water. Drain and cut off the tough stems. There will be about ¾ pound of each green. Cut the leaves into ¼-inch strips. There will be 6 to 8 tightly packed cups.

2. In a well-seasoned wok, heat the olive oil over moderately high heat. Add the garlic and cook, stirring, 30 seconds. Add half of the greens and cook, stirring, for about 1 minute, until they begin to wilt. Add the remaining greens and cook, stirring constantly, for 8 to 10 minutes, until the greens darken slightly and are fairly tender.

3. Season with the salt, pepper, and lemon juice.

Pork Stews

Green Pork Chili with Kale and Hominy

8 to 10 Servings

This is an exceptionally toothsome chili that takes a little meat a long way. Depending upon the heat of the peppers, it can get pretty spicy. Serve with rice and warm tortillas.

3 pounds boneless pork loin

1 pound poblano peppers

1 pound Anaheim peppers

¼ pound lean bacon, chopped

3 medium onions, chopped

6 garlic cloves, chopped

2 teaspoons dried oregano, preferably Mexican

1½ teaspoons ground cumin

3 tablespoons flour

4 cups Simple Meat Stock (page 234), Rich Chicken Stock
    (page 232), or reduced-sodium canned broth

1 tablespoon cider vinegar

1 teaspoon salt

1 bunch of kale (1 to 1½ pounds), tough ends trimmed,
    leaves shredded

1 (15½-ounce) can white hominy, rinsed and drained

1. Trim any external fat from the pork. Cut the meat into 1- by 1½-inch rectangles.

2. Roast the poblano and Anaheim peppers over a charcoal fire or open gas flame or under the broiler as close to the heat as possible, turning, until they are charred all over, 7 to 10 minutes. Remove to a brown paper bag and steam for 10 minutes. Peel the peppers, discarding the stems and seeds, and chop.

3. Preheat the oven to 325 degrees F.

4. In a large flameproof casserole, cook the bacon over moderate heat, stirring occasionally, until it is lightly browned and has given up most of its fat, 5 to 7 minutes. Remove with a slotted spoon and set aside. Add the pork to

the fat in batches without crowding, raise the heat to moderately high, and cook, turning, until lightly browned all over, about 7 minutes per batch. As the meat browns, remove it to a plate.

5. Add the onions to the fat and cook, stirring occasionally, until golden, about 5 minutes. Add the garlic, oregano, and cumin and cook 1 minute longer. Reduce the heat to moderate. Stir in the flour. The mixture will be dry, but continue to cook, stirring, for 1 minute. Stir in the stock and bring to a boil, stirring to scrape up any flour or browned bits from the bottom of the pan. Add the vinegar, salt, and kale. Stir in the reserved bacon and chopped peppers. Return the pork to the pan along with any juices that collect on the plate. Bring to a boil, cover, and transfer to the oven.

6. Bake 1½ hours. Stir in the hominy and bake 30 minutes longer. Season with additional salt to taste.

➤ This stew reheats very well after being refrigerated for a day or two. Stored in a tightly covered container, it will freeze well for up to 3 months.

Pork Stew with Cumin and Smoky Peppers

6 to 8 Servings

A mix of roasted bell and poblano peppers adds color and spice to this light pork stew with its Southwest seasonings. Extra smokiness and heat comes from the chipotle chile. Serve with Mexican Risotto (see page 116) or mashed potatoes.

3 pounds lean pork, cut into 1½-inch cubes

¼ cup extra-virgin olive oil

2 tablespoons fresh lemon juice

1½ teaspoons ground cumin

1½ teaspoons dried Mexican oregano

¼ teaspoon ground allspice

½ teaspoon salt

½ teaspoon freshly ground black pepper

3 garlic cloves, minced

2 red bell peppers

2 yellow bell peppers

1 green bell pepper

2 poblano peppers (or use 1 more green pepper)

2 teaspoons vegetable oil

1 tablespoon cumin seeds

3 cups Rich Chicken Stock (page 232) or reduced-sodium
    canned broth

1½ cups crushed tomatoes

1 teaspoon ground cinnamon

1 dried chipotle chile

1. Trim any excess fat from pork. Place in a bowl and toss with 2 tablespoons of the olive oil, the lemon juice, ground cumin, ½ teaspoon of the oregano, the allspice, salt, black pepper, and 1 minced garlic clove. Set aside at room temperature to marinate 30 to 60 minutes, tossing occasionally.

2. Meanwhile, cut the bell peppers and poblano peppers in half and remove the seeds and stems. Brush the skins with vegetable oil. Grill or broil as close to the heat as possible until charred, 8 to 10 minutes. (Do not place in a bag.) Let cool slightly, then peel off the skins. Cut the roasted peppers into 1½-inch squares.

3. Remove the pork from the marinade and pat dry on paper towels.

4. In a large flameproof casserole, heat the remaining 2 tablespoons extra-virgin olive oil over moderately high heat. Add the pork in 2 batches and cook, turning, until lightly browned, 8 to 10 minutes per batch. As the meat is browned, transfer to a plate.

5. Pour off all but 1 tablespoon fat from the pan. Reduce the heat to moderate. Add the cumin seeds and remaining garlic and cook, stirring, until the cumin is lightly browned and fragrant, 1 to 2 minutes. Add the chicken stock to pan and bring to a boil, scraping up the browned bits from the bottom of the pan. Add the tomatoes, remaining 1 teaspoon oregano, cinnamon, and chipotle chile.

6. Return the pork to the pan along with any juices that have collected on the plate. Cover and simmer over moderately low heat 1 hour, or until the pork is tender. Taste after 30 minutes and remove the chipotle chile if the stew is beginning to taste too hot. When the pork is tender, add the peppers and simmer 5 minutes, until the peppers are just tender but still firm. Season the sauce with additional salt and pepper to taste. If the chipotle is not too hot for your taste, remove it, mince it finely, and return it to the stew; otherwise, discard it before serving.

➤ This stew reheats well after a day or two in the refrigerator. Stored in a tightly covered container, it will freeze well for up to 3 months.

Pork and Sausage Goulash

6 to 8 Servings

*Y*ears ago, a Hungarian friend of mine taught me a wonderful sausage and potato goulash. Recently, a German visitor, Marian Moffat, shared with me a very pristine pork goulash — onions, pork, paprika, sauerkraut, and stock — a recipe she learned from her Hungarian friend Katharina Petery. I put the two together in a most inauthentic but delicious way that makes a hearty one-dish meal that's perfect for a cold fall or winter evening. Serve with chewy sourdough, rye, or pumpernickel bread.

1½ *pounds boneless pork loin*
½ *teaspoon salt*
¼ *teaspoon freshly ground black pepper*
1 *pound smoked Hungarian garlic sausage or kielbasa*
4 *pounds fresh (refrigerated) sauerkraut*
3 *tablespoons goose or duck fat or olive oil*
2 *medium onions, thinly sliced*
3 *tablespoons imported sweet paprika*
2 *tablespoons imported hot paprika*
1 *tablespoon flour*
½ *teaspoon dried thyme leaves*
1½ *pounds red potatoes, peeled and thinly sliced*
⅔ *cup dry white wine*
2 *cups Rich Chicken Stock (page 232) or reduced-sodium*
   canned broth
Sour cream

1. Trim all excess fat from the pork and cut the meat into 1-inch cubes. Season the pork with the salt and pepper. Cut the sausage into ¼-inch slices. Rinse and drain the sauerkraut; squeeze out as much excess moisture as possible.

2. In a large skillet, heat the fat over moderately high heat. Add the pork in 2 batches if necessary, and cook, turning and reducing the heat to moderate if the fat begins to burn, until the meat is lightly browned, 5 to 7 minutes per batch. As the pork browns, remove it to a plate.

3. Add the onions to the skillet, reduce the heat to moderate, cover, and cook 2 minutes. Uncover and cook, stirring occasionally, until they begin to brown, 5 to 7 minutes longer. Sprinkle the sweet and hot paprika and the flour over the onions and cook, stirring, 1 minute. Remove from the heat.

4. Preheat the oven to 350 degrees F.

5. Layer about one third of the sauerkraut in a large flameproof casserole. Add half the browned pork. Sprinkle half the thyme over the meat. Spoon half the onions over the meat. Top with a single layer of sliced potatoes, overlapping slightly, and then a layer of half the sausage. Cover that with half the remaining sauerkraut. Repeat these layers, ending with the remaining sauerkraut.

6. Pour the wine into the skillet the onions were in and bring to a boil, scraping up the brown bits from the bottom of the pan. Pour into the casserole. Pour in enough stock to barely cover. Bring to a boil, transfer to the oven, and bake 1¼ to 1½ hours, until the sauerkraut is tender. Serve with a bowl of sour cream on the side.

➤ This dish keeps in the refrigerator for up to 3 days. Stored in a tightly covered container, it will freeze well for up to 3 months.

Rosemary Ragout of Pork with Zucchini and Sweet Peppers

6 to 8 Servings T*his easy-to-make stew is simple and colorful. Serve over couscous or with Parmesan Polenta Ring (see page 97) and a good Italian red wine.*

> *3 pounds lean pork, cut into 1½- to 2-inch cubes*
> *¼ cup extra-virgin olive oil*
> *2 tablespoons fresh lemon juice*
> *1 teaspoon rosemary*
> *¼ teaspoon ground allspice*
> *1 teaspoon salt*
> *¾ teaspoon freshly ground black pepper*
> *2 garlic cloves, crushed through a press*
> *1 medium onion, finely chopped*
> *⅔ cup dry white wine*
> *2 cups Rich Chicken Stock (page 232) or reduced-sodium*
>   *canned broth*
> *1 cup crushed tomatoes*
> *1 bay leaf*
> *2 red bell peppers (or better yet, 1 red and 1 yellow), roasted,*
>   *peeled, and cut into 1½-inch squares*
> *4 small zucchini, cut into ¾-inch rounds*

1. In a large bowl, marinate the pork in 2 tablespoons of the olive oil with the lemon juice, ½ teaspoon of the rosemary, the allspice, ½ teaspoon salt, ½ teaspoon pepper, and garlic for 2 hours at room temperature or up to 6 hours in the refrigerator.

2. In a large flameproof casserole, heat the remaining 2 tablespoons oil over moderately high heat. Add the pork in 2 batches and cook, turning, until nicely browned, 8 to 10 minutes per batch. Remove the pork to a plate.

3. Add the onion to the casserole, reduce the heat to moderate, and cook, stirring occasionally, until golden, about 5 minutes. Add the wine and bring to a

boil, stirring up the browned bits from the bottom of the pan. Return the pork to the casserole along with any juices that have collected on the plate. Add the chicken stock and crushed tomatoes. Return the pork to the casserole. Add the bay leaf, remaining ½ teaspoon rosemary, remaining ½ teaspoon salt, and remaining ¼ teaspoon freshly ground pepper. Bring to a boil, reduce the heat, cover, and simmer 1 hour. Remove and discard the bay leaf.

4. Add the roasted peppers and zucchini, cover and simmer until the zucchini is just tender, 5 to 7 minutes.

➤ This stew can be made ahead through Step 3 and refrigerated for up to 2 days or frozen for up to 3 months. After adding the peppers and zucchini, it should not be stored or recooked, or the zucchini will give off too much liquid and turn mushy.

Neapolitan Ragout of Sausages and Peppers

6 to 8 Servings

*T*his is a pretty stew, especially if you use the three different-colored peppers. You can throw an orange one in, too, if you like. The trick is to sauté the peppers so that they are almost done, but still brightly colored and slightly crisp. If you are making the stew ahead, add the peppers at the last minute, so they don't overcook.

2 pounds pork or poultry sausage, hot or sweet (I like to use a mix)
3½ tablespoons olive oil
1 large white onion, thickly sliced
3 bell peppers (preferably 1 green, 1 red, and 1 yellow), cut into
*   2-inch pieces*
1 tablespoon chopped garlic
¼ teaspoon crushed hot red pepper
1 teaspoon dried oregano, Sicilian if you have it
1 cup dry red wine
2 cans (28 ounces each) Italian peeled tomatoes, coarsely
*   chopped, juices from 1 can reserved*
2 tablespoons sun-dried tomato tapenade or tomato paste
½ teaspoon salt
¼ teaspoon freshly ground black pepper

1. Prick the sausages all over. In a large flameproof casserole, cook the sausages over moderate heat, turning, until browned all over, 5 to 7 minutes. Remove to a platter; pour off all the fat from the pan.

2. Add 1½ tablespoons olive oil and the onion to the casserole. Cook over moderately high heat, stirring occasionally, until the onion is slightly softened and lightly browned around the edges, about 3 minutes. With a slotted spoon, remove to a bowl. Add another tablespoon of oil and the bell peppers to the pan and cook, tossing, until the peppers are crisp-tender and brightly colored, about 5 minutes. Remove to the bowl with the onion.

3. Add the remaining 1 tablespoon oil to the pan and reduce the heat to moderately low. Add the garlic and cook until softened and fragrant, 1 to 2 minutes. Add the crushed hot pepper, oregano, and wine and boil until the wine is reduced by half, about 3 minutes. Add the tomatoes with the reserved juice, sun-dried tomato tapenade, salt, and freshly ground pepper. Bring to a boil, reduce the heat to moderately low, and simmer, partially covered, stirring occasionally, until the tomatoes soften and the sauce thickens slightly, about 20 minutes.

4. Cut the sausages into 2-inch lengths and add them to the sauce, along with any juices that have collected on the platter. Simmer, partially covered, 10 minutes, or until the sausages are cooked through. The recipe can be made to this point up to 2 days ahead.

5. Just before serving, return the casserole to a simmer. Add the onion and peppers along with any juices that have collected in the bowl, cover, and simmer 3 to 5 minutes longer, until the peppers are just barely tender but still bright colored.

➤ This stew can be prepared through Step 4 up to 2 days in advance, and in truth, can even be reheated with the peppers and onion, but in that case they will lose their texture. I do not freeze it.

Braised Chinese Spareribs with Black Beans and Garlic

4 to 6 Servings

To turn this traditional Chinese preparation for spareribs into a stew, I merely added some extra vegetables and liquid. For people who share my love for fermented black beans and garlic, this is an irresistible dish. So that the meat can be picked up easily, the slabs of ribs must be cut crosswise into 1- to 1½-inch pieces; ask your butcher to do this. Serve with lots of rice or Chinese noodles.

> 3½ to 4 pounds pork spareribs, cut crosswise into
>   1- to 1½-inch lengths
> 2 medium-large white onions
> 2 large green bell peppers
> 6 garlic cloves
> ¼ cup fermented black beans
> 1 teaspoon minced fresh ginger
> ¼ to ½ teaspoon crushed hot red pepper
> 3 tablespoons vegetable oil
> 2 tablespoons soy sauce
> 1 tablespoon dry sherry
> 2 teaspoons brown sugar
> 1½ teaspoons cornstarch dissolved in ¼ cup water

1. Trim off any excess fat from the spareribs and cut between the bones to separate the ribs. Cut the onions in half crosswise; then cut each half into 6 wedges to make triangular wedges about 1½ to 2 inches. Do the same with the green peppers, cutting each half into 4 or 6 wedges, depending on size. Set the vegetables aside separately.

2. Coarsely chop the garlic. Add the black beans and chop together until the garlic is finely chopped. Blend in the ginger and hot pepper.

3. In a large flameproof casserole, heat 2 tablespoons of the oil over moderately high heat. Add the onions and sauté 2 minutes. Add the green peppers and sauté 2 to 3 minutes longer, until the vegetables are crisp-tender and the peppers are bright green. Remove with a slotted spoon and set aside.

4. Add the remaining 1 tablespoon oil and the ribs to the same casserole and cook, stirring often, until the ribs are no longer pink, about 7 minutes. Remove them with a slotted spoon and pour off all but 1 tablespoon fat from the pan. Reduce the heat to moderate. Add the garlic-black bean mixture and cook, stirring, 1 minute. Pour in 2½ cups of water and return the ribs to the pan. Add the soy sauce, sherry, and brown sugar. Bring to a boil, cover, reduce the heat to low, and simmer 45 to 55 minutes, or until the ribs are very tender.

5. Remove the ribs and skim off as much fat as possible from the sauce. Stir the dissolved cornstarch into the sauce and bring to a boil, stirring until thickened and clear, 1 to 2 minutes. Return the ribs to the pan and gently stir the onions and peppers into the stew. Partially cover and simmer 5 minutes, stirring once or twice.

➤ Stored in a tightly covered container, this stew can be refrigerated for up to 3 days or frozen for up to 3 months, though the peppers will lose their texture and color.

Braised Lentils with Kielbasa and Mushrooms

6 to 8 Servings

*T*he earthiness of the mushrooms and lentils here provide a lovely balance to the sausage. Use a deep red wine, such as a cabernet. For best flavor, it's worth a trip to a butcher or specialty market for a freshly made, lightly smoked kielbasa.

½ ounce imported dried mushrooms

3 tablespoons olive oil

2 medium onions, chopped

2 celery ribs, chopped

1 medium carrot, chopped

3 garlic cloves, minced

12 ounces fresh white mushrooms, sliced

1½ cups dry red wine

4 cups Simple Meat Stock (page 234), Rich Chicken Stock
    (page 232), or reduced-sodium canned broth

3 plum tomatoes, peeled, seeded, and diced

¼ cup chopped parsley

½ teaspoon dried thyme leaves

1 bay leaf

1 teaspoon salt

½ teaspoon freshly ground black pepper

1 pound lentils, rinsed and picked over

2 pounds lightly smoked kielbasa, cut diagonally into 1½- to
    2-inch lengths

1. In a heatproof bowl, soak the dried mushrooms in 1 cup of boiling water until soft, about 15 minutes. Squeeze excess liquid from the mushrooms back into the bowl and chop the mushrooms. Strain and reserve the soaking water.

2. Meanwhile, in a large flameproof casserole, heat the oil over moderately low heat. Add the onions, cover, and cook 2 minutes. Uncover, add the celery, carrot, and garlic and cook, stirring occasionally, until all the vegetables are softened, 8 to 10 minutes.

3. Add the fresh mushrooms to the casserole, raise the heat to moderate, and cook, stirring often, until the mushrooms give up their liquid, about 5 minutes. Add the chopped dried mushrooms and cook 1 minute longer.

4. Add the wine and bring to a boil; boil for 2 minutes. Add the stock, tomatoes, reserved mushroom soaking water, 2 tablespoons of the parsley, the thyme, bay leaf, salt, and pepper. Add the lentils and simmer, partially covered, stirring up the lentils from the bottom of the pot once or twice, for 30 minutes. Add the kielbasa and simmer until the lentils are tender but not falling apart, 10 to 15 minutes longer. Stir in the remaining parsley. Remove and discard the bay leaf before serving.

➤ This dish will keep well in the refrigerator for up to 3 days, though you may have to add some extra liquid when you reheat it, because the lentils will continue to absorb the moisture. Because it is a very thick stew, I prefer not to freeze it.

Lion's Head Casserole

6 Servings
Lion's Head is a homey Chinese dish of very large pork meatballs served on a bed of bok choy. When mixed with some additional varieties of vegetables for added color, flavor, and crunch, it makes a lovely stew, which needs only a bowl of white rice to accompany it.

- 2 pounds lean ground pork
- 4½ tablespoons dark (black) soy sauce
- 3 tablespoons ice water
- 1½ tablespoons pale dry sherry
- ¼ cup plus 2 tablespoons cornstarch
- 2½ teaspoons brown sugar
- 2 tablespoons minced white of scallion
- 3½ teaspoons finely minced fresh ginger
- 4 garlic cloves, crushed through a press
- 1 ounce Chinese dried black mushrooms
- 3 tablespoons peanut oil
- 1 medium-large head of bok choy (1½ to 2 pounds), stems halved lengthwise and cut into 1½-inch pieces, leaves halved and cut into wide strips
- ¼ pound snow peas, stemmed and stringed
- 1 (8-ounce) can drained whole water chestnuts, cut in half if large

1. In a medium bowl, combine the ground pork with 3 tablespoons soy sauce, the ice water, sherry, 1½ tablespoons cornstarch, 1½ teaspoons brown sugar, the minced scallions, 2 teaspoons of the ginger, and half the garlic. Mix with your hands to blend well. Let stand for 20 to 30 minutes.

2. Meanwhile, in a medium heatproof bowl, soak the dried mushrooms in 1 cup boiling water until soft, about 20 minutes. Remove the mushrooms one at a time and squeeze the liquid back into the bowl. Cut off the stems and halve or quarter the mushroom caps, depending on size. Strain and reserve the soaking liquid.

3. Put ¼ cup of the cornstarch in a shallow bowl. Form the seasoned ground pork into 6 large meatballs and roll in the cornstarch to coat.

4. In a large skillet, heat 2 tablespoons of the oil over moderately high heat. Add the meatballs and cook, turning gently, until browned all over, about 5 minutes. Reduce the heat to moderate if the bottom of the pan begins to burn. Use a wide metal spatula to turn the meatballs, which will be soft. When the meatballs are browned, carefully remove them to a large flameproof casserole.

5. Add the remaining 1 tablespoon oil and the bok choy to the skillet and stir-fry 2 minutes to soften slightly. Remove to a bowl and set aside.

6. Pour 1½ cups of water over the meatballs in the casserole. Add the remaining 1½ tablespoons soy sauce, 1 teaspoon brown sugar, 1½ teaspoons ginger, remaining garlic, and the reserved mushroom soaking liquid. Bring to a boil, reduce the heat to low, cover, and simmer for 1 hour.

7. In a medium saucepan of boiling water, cook the snow peas until bright green but still crisp, about 1 minute. Drain and rinse under cold running water; drain well.

8. With a slotted skimmer or large spoon, carefully remove the meatballs to a plate. Add the bok choy with any juices in the bowl to the casserole. Set the meatballs on top. Add the Chinese mushrooms and simmer 10 minutes. Add the snow peas and water chestnuts and simmer 1 to 2 minutes to heat through.

9. Remove the meatballs and vegetables to a serving dish. Dissolve the remaining 1½ teaspoons cornstarch in 1 or 2 tablespoons cold water and stir into the sauce in the pan. Bring to a boil, stirring until thickened and smooth, 1 to 2 minutes. Pour the sauce over the vegetables and serve at once. Or return the meatballs and vegetables to the sauce and reheat before serving.

➤ Because of the large amount of bok choy, which is a variety of cabbage, this dish really does not store well, and I would not freeze it.

Lamb Stews

Lamb, an assertive meat, is the perfect foil for any number of spices, herbs, fruits, and vegetables and is used to create a wide variety of tasty stews. With the exception of certain parts of the United States where it is sadly unappreciated and hard to come by, lamb is popular everywhere it is raised, from France and Ireland to China and the Middle East. These days a good deal of our lamb comes from both New Zealand and Australia, some from animals who are free-ranging and antibiotic free. But because of the plastic vacuum packaging they are shipped in, the length of time they remain on the shelf, and the long distances they travel — often in a frozen state — I prefer the flavor of young, fresh American lamb, much of which comes from Colorado.

As with beef and pork, I have chosen to develop these lamb stews with lean meat — mainly from the leg. While leg of lamb is much more expensive than shank or neck, which is often sold as lamb stew meat, there is so little waste and so much less shrinkage that the economic difference is not as great as it appears at first glance. And getting the fat off the meat also removes some of the gamier taste

of older lamb, which puts off some people. If you take the trouble to trim it well, you will be surprised at how lean lamb becomes.

A whole leg of lamb will usually weigh six and a half to seven pounds and will yield about five pounds of trimmed meat. To save preparation time, I often buy a whole leg and cut up all the meat at once. I use half the meat immediately and freeze the remainder for my next lamb stew.

Lamb stew made from the leg can take anywhere from half an hour to an hour and a half to cook, depending upon the size of the chunks and the mix of seasonings and accompaniments. It will almost invariably taste better reheated. In this chapter, lamb is paired with spring vegetables in a classic navarin, with prunes and dried cranberries and apricots in Fruited Lamb Curry with Almonds and Mint, and with beans in Oven-Baked Lamb Stew with White Beans and Savory.

Lamb Stew au Ratatouille

4 to 6 Servings

*I*f you don't like cutting up meat, ask your butcher to bone and cube the lamb for you; be sure he saves the bones. The most important thing here is not to overcook the vegetables; so if you are making the stew ahead, stop it as soon as you add the lamb to the ratatouille. Done this way, the stew improves upon standing.*

1 (3- to 3½-pound) shank half leg of lamb,

4 medium onions

1 bay leaf

½ teaspoon dried thyme leaves

4 large sprigs of parsley

6 garlic cloves, 3 bruised, 3 whole

3 tablespoons vegetable oil

¾ cup dry white wine

3 tablespoons extra-virgin olive oil

1 pound medium-small zucchini, halved lengthwise and cut into
    1-inch dice

1 medium eggplant (about 1 pound), peeled and cut into
    1-inch dice

2 bell peppers, preferably 1 green and 1 red, cut into
    1-inch squares

1 pound fresh plum tomatoes, peeled, seeded, and coarsely
    chopped or 1 (14-ounce) can Italian peeled tomatoes,
    drained and chopped

1 teaspoon salt

½ teaspoon freshly ground black pepper

⅛ teaspoon cayenne

1 ½ tablespoons balsamic vinegar

1 tablespoon lemon juice

1 tablespoon dried tomato pesto

½ cup coarsely chopped fresh basil (see Note)

1. Bone the leg of lamb. Set the bones aside. Cut the meat into 1-inch cubes. Trim off and discard any external fat or connective tissue.

2. Thinly slice 2 of the onions. Cut the remaining onions into ¾-inch dice. Tie the bay leaf, thyme, parsley, and bruised garlic in a cheesecloth bag.

3. In a large flameproof casserole, heat 2 tablespoons of the vegetable oil over moderately high heat. Add the lamb and the bones in 2 batches and cook, turning, until nicely browned, about 7 minutes per batch. Remove to a plate.

4. Add the remaining 1 tablespoon vegetable oil and the sliced onions to the casserole and cook until they are very soft and golden brown, 5 to 7 minutes. Add the wine and bring to a boil, scraping up the browned bits from the bottom of the pan. Return the lamb and bones to the pot along with any juices on the plate. Add the cheesecloth bag and 4 cups of water, or enough to barely cover the meat and bones. Partially cover the pot and simmer, skimming occasionally, 1¼ hours, or until the lamb is tender. Drain into a colander set over a bowl; discard the bones and cheesecloth bag. Measure the juices. If there is more than 1½ cups, boil to reduce; if there is less, add water to make up the difference.

5. Meanwhile, in another large flameproof casserole, heat the olive oil over moderately high heat. Add the diced onions and cook, stirring occasionally, until they soften and begin to color, 5 to 7 minutes. Add the zucchini, eggplant, and bell peppers and cook, stirring frequently, for 5 minutes. Add the tomatoes, salt, black pepper, and cayenne. Cook until the vegetables are just barely tender, about 5 minutes longer. Stir in the vinegar, lemon juice, and dried tomato pesto.

6. Add the lamb and reduced lamb juices to the vegetables. Crush the remaining 3 garlic cloves through a press into the stew and simmer 5 minutes. Stir in the chopped basil and season with additional salt and pepper to taste.

◇ **Note:** If you don't have fresh basil, add 1 teaspoon dried basil to the stew along with the tomatoes; toss in ¼ cup chopped parsley at the end.

➤ Stored in a tightly closed container, this can refrigerated for up to 2 days or frozen for up to 3 months, but the vegetables will lose texture.

Lamb Curry with Ginger and Tomatoes

4 to 6 Servings A*lthough in many stews the meat is often cut into large chunks, here the lamb should be in small pieces to enable it to cook until tender in a relatively short time, so that the spices remain vibrant.*

1½ pounds fresh plum tomatoes or 1 (28-ounce) can Italian
  peeled tomatoes, drained and chopped
1 (2½- to 3-pound) boneless leg of lamb or lean lamb shoulder
3 tablespoons vegetable oil
2 medium onions, thinly sliced
4 garlic cloves, minced
1½ tablespoons ground coriander
1 teaspoon ground cumin
½ teaspoon turmeric
¼ teaspoon ground cardamom
¼ teaspoon cayenne
⅛ teaspoon grated nutmeg
Pinch of saffron threads
1 tablespoon plus 1 teaspoon grated fresh ginger
1 teaspoon salt
2 cups Simple Meat Stock (page 234) or water

1. If using fresh tomatoes, bring a large saucepan of water to a boil. Drop in the tomatoes and boil for 10 seconds, or until the skin begins to pucker. Drain into a colander and rinse under cold running water. Peel off the skins. Halve the tomatoes and squeeze out the seeds. Coarsely chop the tomatoes.

2. Trim all excess fat from the lamb and cut the meat into 1-inch cubes. In a large flameproof casserole, heat the oil over moderately high heat. Add the lamb in 2 batches and sauté until nicely browned, about 7 minutes per batch. As the meat browns, transfer to a plate.

3. Add the onions to the pan, reduce the heat to moderate, and cook, stirring occasionally, until they are soft and beginning to turn golden, 5 to 7 minutes.

Add the garlic and sprinkle on the coriander, cumin, turmeric, cardamom, cayenne, nutmeg, and saffron. Cook, stirring constantly, 1 to 2 minutes to toast the spices. Stir in the tomatoes, ginger, and salt.

4. Return the lamb to the pan, along with any juices that have collected on the plate. Pour in the stock. Bring to a boil, reduce the heat to moderately low, cover, and simmer 30 to 40 minutes, until the lamb is very tender and the sauce is slightly reduced.

➤ Stored in a tightly closed container, this stew can be refrigerated for up to 3 days or frozen for up to 3 months. However, the flavor will not be quite as intense as when it is just cooked.

Lamb Stews

Fruited Lamb Curry with Almonds and Mint

4 to 6 Servings

L*amb's richness pairs well with both spices and fruits, particularly the dried fruits called for here. If you want to serve this stew for a party, know that the recipe doubles easily. Serve with basmati or wild rice.*

2 pounds boneless leg of lamb, cut into 1½-inch cubes

3 medium onions

½ cup plain nonfat yogurt

1½ tablespoons ground coriander

1 teaspoon ground cumin

1 teaspoon salt

¾ teaspoon ground cinnamon

½ teaspoon freshly ground black pepper

½ teaspoon ground cardamom

¼ teaspoon ground cloves

¼ to ½ teaspoon cayenne, to taste

1 tablespoon minced fresh ginger

3 garlic cloves, minced

1½ tablespoons butter (or use all oil)

1½ tablespoons vegetable oil

2 tablespoons cider vinegar

⅓ cup slivered almonds

½ cup dried cranberries (about 2 ounces)

½ cup raisins, preferably Muscat

½ cup dried apricots

½ cup pitted prunes

1 tablespoon fresh lemon juice

¼ cup chopped fresh mint

1. Trim any excess fat from the lamb and place in a medium bowl. Quarter one of the onions; slice the other two.

2. In a food processor, combine the quartered onion with the yogurt, coriander, cumin, salt, cinnamon, pepper, cardamom, cloves, cayenne, ginger, and garlic. Puree until smooth. Pour over the lamb and toss to mix. Let stand 1 to 2 hours at room temperature.

3. In a large flameproof casserole, melt the butter in the oil over moderate heat. Add the sliced onions and cook, stirring occasionally, until they are soft and golden, 6 to 8 minutes. Pour in the lamb with its marinade and cook, stirring, until the lamb is no longer pink, about 7 minutes. Add 3½ cups water and the vinegar and bring to a simmer. Reduce the heat to moderately low, cover, and cook 1 hour.

4. Meanwhile, in a medium dry skillet, toss the almonds over moderate heat until they are lightly toasted, 4 to 5 minutes.

5. After 1 hour, add the toasted almonds, dried cranberries, raisins, apricots, and prunes to the stew and simmer, uncovered, 10 minutes, or until the fruit is plump and soft but still intact. (If you're making this stew ahead — and it does reheat well — remove it from the heat as soon as you add the fruit. It will plump up upon standing and reheating.)

6. Just before serving, stir the lemon juice and 3 tablespoons of the chopped mint into the stew. Serve with the remaining mint sprinkled on top.

➤ This stew reheats well after up to 2 days in the refrigerator. Stored in a tightly closed container, it will freeze well for up to 6 months.

Greek Lamb with Green Beans and Garlic-Roasted Potatoes

6 to 8 Servings

*H*ere's my version of lamb kampama, *a traditional Greek stew. I've given a little twist of garlic-roasted potatoes to this one-pot meal. If you wish to omit this extra step, simply add cut-up red potatoes to the stew during the last half-hour of cooking.*

5½ to 6 pounds leg of lamb, boned, meat cut into 1½ to 2-inch cubes (4 ¾ pounds trimmed meat)
Salt
Freshly ground black pepper
3 tablespoons olive oil
2 tablespoons butter
2 medium onions, chopped
12 garlic cloves, 3 minced, 9 whole with skins left on
1½ cups dry white wine
1 (28-ounce) can Italian peeled tomatoes, drained and pureed
2 cinnamon sticks
½ teaspoon dried oregano
⅛ teaspoon ground allspice
1 bay leaf
2 pounds small red potatoes, peeled and halved
1 tablespoon extra-virgin olive oil
1 ¼ pounds green beans

1. Trim any excess fat and connective tissue from the meat. Season generously with salt and pepper. In a large flameproof casserole, heat 2 tablespoons of the olive oil over moderately high heat. Add the lamb in 2 or 3 batches and sauté, turning, until nicely browned all over, 5 to 7 minutes per batch. As the lamb browns, remove it to a plate. Pour out any fat left in the pan.

2. Melt the butter in the remaining 1 tablespoon olive oil. Add the onions and cook over moderate heat, stirring occasionally, until golden, 5 to 7 minutes. Add the minced garlic and cook 1 minute longer.

3. Pour in the wine and the pureed tomatoes. Add the cinnamon sticks, oregano, allspice, bay leaf, 1 teaspoon salt, and ½ teaspoon pepper. Return the lamb to the casserole along with any juices that have collected on the plate. Bring to a simmer, cover, reduce the heat to low and cook 1¼ hours.

4. Meanwhile, preheat the oven to 400 degrees F.

5. Place the potatoes in a small roasting pan or shallow baking dish, drizzle on the extra-virgin olive oil, and toss to coat. Scatter the garlic cloves around the dish, cover the dish with foil, and roast for 20 minutes. Turn the potatoes and roast uncovered 20 to 25 minutes longer, or until the potatoes are lightly browned. Discard the garlic (it will be bitter at this point because it has roasted at such a high temperature for so long).

6. Add the green beans to the lamb and simmer 15 minutes. Add the potatoes and cook 5 to 10 minutes longer.

➤ Though the green beans lose their color, this stew tastes very good when reheated after a few hours, or even after being refrigerated overnight. However, because the potatoes and green beans will lose their texture, I do not freeze it.

Lamb Stews

Hunan Lamb Stew with Leeks

6 to 8 Servings

Usually seen as a stir-fried dish,
*this duo of lamb and leeks becomes a lovely light stew with these aromatic
Asian seasonings added. Serve with a big bowl of steamed white rice.*

1 (2½ to 3-pound) boneless leg of lamb

4 medium leeks

3 tablespoons vegetable oil

¼ cup thin Chinese soy sauce

¼ cup dry sherry

1 tablespoon red wine vinegar

2 tablespoons packed dark brown sugar

4 garlic cloves, crushed through a press

5 star anise pods

½ to 1 teaspoon crushed hot red pepper, to taste

3 large strips of orange zest

2 teaspoons cornstarch

1. Trim all excess fat from the lamb and cut the meat into 2 by 1-inch
rectangles. Trim the roots off the leeks and cut off only the very top parts of
the green. Rinse the leeks well, split lengthwise, and rinse again. Cut the white
and green into 2-inch lengths.

2. In a large flameproof casserole, heat 2 tablespoons of the oil over
moderately high heat. Add the lamb in batches without crowding and cook, turning, until nicely browned, about 7 minutes per batch. As the meat browns,
remove it to a plate.

3. Add the remaining 1 tablespoon oil and the white and green of the
leeks to the pan, reduce the heat to moderate, and cook, stirring occasionally,
until wilted but not browned, 3 to 5 minutes. Add 2 cups of water to the pan and
bring to a boil, stirring up any browned bits from the bottom of the pan. Return
the lamb to the casserole along with any juices that have accumulated on the
plate. Add the soy sauce, sherry, vinegar, brown sugar, and garlic. Tie the star
anise, hot pepper, and orange zest in cheesecloth and add to the pot.

4. Cover, reduce the heat to moderately low, and simmer 1 hour, or until the lamb is very tender. Dissolve the cornstarch in 2 tablespoons water and stir into the pot. Bring to a boil, stirring until the sauce is slightly thickened, 1 to 2 minutes.

➤ This stew is even better reheated after a day or two in the refrigerator. Stored in a tightly covered container, it will freeze well for up to 6 months.

Lamb Stews

Oven-Baked Lamb Stew with White Beans and Savory

16 to 20 Servings

In France, this dish would be made with flageolets—delicate, pale green, thin oval beans. If you can find them, use them; if not, the small white navy beans called for work well. This recipe improves if made a day or two ahead and reheated, so that the flavors have a chance to permeate the beans.

2 pounds dried navy beans or flageolets

3 medium onions, chopped

2 medium carrots, chopped

1 celery rib with leaves, chopped

1½ tablespoons minced fresh savory or 1 teaspoon dried, crumbled

2 bay leaves

2 whole cloves

5½ to 6 pounds leg of lamb, boned, trimmed, and cut into 1½-inch cubes (about 4 pounds of meat)

Salt

Freshly ground black pepper

¼ cup olive oil

¼ pound lean salt pork, finely diced

8 garlic cloves, finely chopped

1 cup dry white wine

1 (28-ounce) can Italian peeled tomatoes, drained and chopped

2 cups Simple Meat Stock (page 234) or Brown Chicken Stock (page 233)

½ cup chopped Italian parsley

1. Rinse the beans, pick over to remove any pebbles or grit, and soak in a large bowl of cold water overnight. Drain the beans and rinse well. Place in a stockpot and add 1 chopped onion, 1 chopped carrot, the celery, and 1½ teaspoons of the fresh savory or ½ teaspoon dried.

2. Tie 1 of the bay leaves and the cloves in a small piece of cheesecloth and add to the pot. Pour in enough cold water to cover by about ½ inch and boil until the beans are tender, 45 to 60 minutes, or longer if necessary. Ladle out 2 cups of the bean water. Drain the beans into a colander; discard the cheesecloth bag.

3. Meanwhile, trim excess fat from the lamb. Season with salt and pepper.

4. In a very large (8- to 9-quart) flameproof casserole, heat 3 tablespoons of the olive oil. Add the salt pork and cook over moderate heat, stirring occasionally, until lightly browned, 5 to 7 minutes. With a slotted spoon, remove to a bowl and set aside. Raise the heat to moderately high. Add the lamb in 1 or 2 batches and cook, turning, until nicely browned, 8 to 10 minutes per batch. As it browns, remove the lamb to a plate.

5. Add the remaining 1 tablespoon oil and chopped onions to the casserole, reduce the heat to moderate and cook, stirring occasionally, until the onions are golden and beginning to brown, about 7 minutes. Add the remaining carrot, 4 of the garlic cloves, and the remaining savory and cook, stirring often, until the vegetables are softened, about 3 minutes.

6. Pour in the wine and bring to a boil, scraping up any brown bits from the bottom of the pan. Add the tomatoes, the stock, the remaining bay leaf, ½ teaspoon salt, and ¾ teaspoon pepper. Return the lamb to the pot along with any juices that have collected on the plate and the salt pork. Bring to a boil, reduce the heat to low, cover, and simmer 40 minutes. Remove and discard the bay leaf. Preheat the oven to 325 degrees F.

7. Add the beans to the lamb. If the stew seems too dry, add ½ to 1 cup of the reserved bean liquid. (The recipe can be prepared to this point up to 2 days in advance.) Bring to a simmer, cover, and transfer to the oven. Bake 1 hour. Uncover and bake 30 to 45 minutes, or until most of the liquid is absorbed and what is left is thickened and soupy. (Add a little more of the reserved bean liquid if the mixture seems to be drying out.) Shortly before serving, stir in the parsley and the remaining garlic.

➤ This dish reheats well after a day or two in the refrigerator: let return to room temperature, then reheat in a 325 degree F. oven for 35 to 45 minutes, until hot throughout. I don't like to freeze beans because they become mushy.

Ragout of Lamb and Sweet Peppers with Basil and Mint

6 Servings

My friend Marge Poore, author of *365 Easy Mexican Recipes, gave me the recipe for this savory ragout with its soupy sauce. Reflective of Northern California, where Marge and her husband, Bill, live, it is light and fresh-tasting, with Mediterranean overtones. Serve over rice or, better yet, over couscous tossed with currants and slivered almonds.*

2½ to 3 pounds boneless leg of lamb, cut into 1- to 1½-inch cubes
Salt
Freshly ground black pepper
¼ cup olive oil
⅔ cup dry white wine
¾ pound small white boiling onions, peeled (see Note, *page 15)*
*2 cups Simple Meat Stock (page 234) or reduced-sodium canned
    chicken broth*
2 teaspoons soy sauce
2 bay leaves
1 tablespoon imported sweet paprika
½ teaspoon dried thyme leaves
*1 large ripe tomato, peeled, seeded, and chopped or 1¼ cups
    drained chopped canned tomatoes*
1 tablespoon fresh lemon juice
2 tablespoons slivered fresh mint
1 large red bell pepper, cut into 2 by ¼-inch strips
1 large yellow bell pepper, cut into 2 by ¼-inch strips
2 tablespoons slivered fresh basil

1. Preheat the oven to 325 degrees F.

2. Trim any excess fat from the meat and pat dry with paper towels. Season lightly with salt and pepper.

3. In a large flameproof casserole, heat 3 tablespoons of the olive oil over moderate heat. Add the lamb in 2 or 3 batches and cook, turning, until browned all over, 5 to 7 minutes per batch. As it browns, remove the meat to a plate.

4. Pour the wine into the pan and bring to a boil, scraping up any brown bits from the bottom of the pan with a wooden spoon. Add the onions, stock, soy sauce, bay leaves, paprika, thyme, tomato, lemon juice, and mint. Bring to a boil. Return the lamb to the casserole along with any juices that have collected on the plate. Cover and transfer to the oven. Bake 45 minutes, or until the lamb and onions are tender.

5. Meanwhile, in a large skillet, heat the remaining 1 tablespoon olive oil. Add the bell peppers and sauté over moderately high heat, stirring frequently, until they are crisp-tender, about 4 minutes. If you make the stew ahead, set aside the lamb and peppers separately.

6. To serve, reheat the lamb ragout if necessary. Remove and discard the bay leaf. Stir in the peppers and transfer to a deep platter or large shallow serving bowl. Sprinkle the fresh basil over the top.

➤ This stew reheats nicely after a day or two in the refrigerator. Stored in a tightly closed container, it can be frozen for up to 6 months, but it will be better if you can add the peppers at the end.

Lamb Stew with Spring Vegetables

6 Servings

Called a navarin *in French, this dish is made for springtime, with the freshest, sweetest vegetables and mild young lamb. It's fine to make this stew ahead. Just be sure to add the sugar snap peas at the last moment so they stay crisp and maintain their bright green color.*

2½ to 3 pounds boneless leg of lamb

Salt and freshly ground black pepper

3 tablespoons olive oil

10 ounces large pearl or small boiling onions, 1 inch in diameter, peeled (see Note, *page 15)*

1 large onion, chopped

1 tablespoon flour

1 cup dry white wine

1 cup chopped peeled and seeded plum tomatoes (2 or 3)

3 cups Simple Meat Stock (page 234) or canned beef broth

½ teaspoon dried thyme leaves

1 bay leaf

1 small head of garlic, separated into cloves and peeled

¾ pound peeled baby carrots

¾ pound baby turnips or halved small

½ pound sugar snap peas

1. Trim any excess fat from the lamb and cut into 1½-inch cubes. Pat dry with paper towels. Season with salt and pepper.

2. In a large flameproof casserole, heat the oil over moderately high heat. Add the pearl onions and cook, turning, until browned, about 7 minutes. Remove with a slotted spoon.

3. Add the lamb in 2 or 3 batches and cook, turning, until nicely browned, 5 to 7 minutes per batch. As the meat browns, transfer it to a plate. Add the chopped onion to the casserole, reduce the heat to moderate and cook, stirring occasionally, until soft and golden brown, about 5 minutes.

4. Add the flour and cook, stirring, for 1 minute. Pour in the wine and bring to a boil. Return the lamb to the pot, along with any juices that have collected on the plate. Add the tomatoes, stock, thyme, and bay leaf. Cover the pot, reduce the heat to moderately low, and cook 25 minutes.

5. Add the garlic cloves, pearl onions, carrots, and turnips to the stew, partially cover, and simmer 30 minutes.

6. Meanwhile, in a large saucepan of boiling salted water, cook the sugar snap peas until bright green and just tender, about 2 minutes. Drain and rinse under cold running water; drain well. When the lamb is ready, add the sugar snap peas. Season the stew with salt and pepper to taste.

➤ Because of the delicate flavor of the broth and the freshness of the vegetables that are integral to this dish, I prefer to serve it shortly after it is made. The stew can be reheated, even frozen for up to 3 months, but the vegetables will lose their texture and color.

Lamb Stews

Lamb and Eggplant Stew
Agrodolce

6 Servings

*A*grodolce *means sweet-and-sour in Italian, and it is a classic with eggplant. Since eggplant and lamb go so well together, I thought the whole combination belonged in a stew. Serve with couscous or rice.*

2½ to 3 pounds boneless leg of lamb
Salt
Freshly ground black pepper
2 medium eggplants (1 pound each)
⅓ cup plus 2 tablespoons olive oil
4 garlic cloves, minced
¼ cup balsamic vinegar
¼ cup red wine vinegar
1 tablespoon sugar
3 cups Simple Meat Stock (page 234) or reduced-sodium
*   canned broth*
½ cup currants
1 tablespoon tomato paste
1 imported bay leaf
¼ cup pine nuts
⅓ cup chopped Italian parsley

1. Trim any external fat and membrane from the lamb and cut the meat into 1-inch pieces. Season lightly with salt and pepper.

2. Rinse and dry the eggplants. Cut off the stems and tips and peel. Cut the eggplant into 1-inch cubes.

3. In a large flameproof casserole, heat ⅓ cup of the olive oil over moderately high heat. Add the lamb in 2 batches and cook, turning, until nicely browned, about 8 minutes per batch. Remove to a bowl and set aside.

4. Add the eggplant to the fat in the pan, cover, reduce the heat to moderate, and cook, stirring occasionally, for 5 minutes. With a slotted spoon, add the eggplant to the bowl with the lamb.

5. Heat the remaining 2 tablespoons olive oil in the same casserole over moderate heat. Add the garlic and cook until softened and fragrant, about 1 minute. Pour in the balsamic vinegar, red wine vinegar, and sugar and boil until reduced by half, about 2 minutes. Add the stock and ½ teaspoon each salt and pepper. Return the eggplant and lamb to the pan, along with any juices that have collected in the bowl. Add the currants, tomato paste, and bay leaf, cover, and simmer 30 minutes. Uncover and simmer 15 minutes longer, or until the lamb is tender and the sauce has reduced and thickened slightly.

6. Meanwhile, in a medium dry skillet, toast the pine nuts over moderate heat, shaking the pan often, until they are lightly browned, about 2 minutes. When the stew is done, remove and discard the bay leaf. Season with additional salt and freshly ground pepper to taste. Stir in the toasted pine nuts and ¼ cup of the chopped parsley. Serve with the remaining parsley sprinkled on top.

➤ The flavor of this dish mellows nicely if it is reheated the next day. Stored in a tightly closed container, it will freeze well for up to 3 months.

Leftover Lamb Stew

6 to 8 Servings T*his tasty recipe, from my dear friend the sculptor Pamela Kelly, uses leftover roast leg of lamb and lots of vegetables to create a stew that's healthy in its carbohydrate balance and full of flavor. The exact amount of meat is not important, since the emphasis here is on the vegetables.*

> *3 large red potatoes, peeled and cut into 1-inch chunks*
> *Bones and cubed meat left over from a whole roast leg of lamb*
> *2 tablespoons olive oil*
> *1 medium onion, chopped*
> *5 garlic cloves, chopped*
> *12 fresh plum tomatoes, peeled, seeded, and coarsely chopped or*
> *   1 (28-ounce) can peeled plum tomatoes, drained and coarsely*
> *   chopped*
> *1½ tablespoons chopped fresh oregano or 1½ teaspoons dried*
> *1 teaspoon sugar*
> *2 medium eggplants, peeled and cut into 1-inch chunks*
> *3 small zucchini, cut into ½-inch rounds*
> *1 red bell pepper, cut into ½-inch squares*
> *1 tablespoon fresh lemon juice*
> *1 (16-ounce) can black beans, rinsed and drained*
> *Salt*
> *Freshly ground black pepper*

1. Boil the potatoes in a large saucepan containing 2 quarts of lightly salted water until just tender, 10 to 12 minutes. Remove the potatoes with a slotted spoon and set aside. Add the lamb bones to the water and boil slowly, skimming occasionally, 25 to 30 minutes; strain. Skim off as much fat as possible from the surface of the broth. The liquid should be reduced to about 4 cups. If there is less, add water; if there is more, boil to reduce.

2. In a large flameproof casserole, heat the oil over moderately high heat. Add the onion and sauté until it is soft and beginning to turn golden, about 5 minutes. Add the garlic and cook until softened and fragrant, 1 to 2 minutes

longer. Stir in the chopped tomatoes, oregano, sugar, eggplant, and lamb-potato broth. Cover partially and cook over moderate heat, stirring occasionally, until the eggplant is just tender, 10 to 15 minutes.

3. Add the zucchini, red pepper, potato chunks, and cubed roast lamb to the pot. Cook 5 to 10 minutes longer, until all the vegetables are tender.

4. Stir in the lemon juice and black beans. Season with salt and pepper to taste.

Fish and Shellfish Stews

We have long enjoyed the pleasure of seafood stews in the form of chunky chowders and gumbos, which bridge the gap between a soup and a stew, and in a few popular classics, such as cioppino and bouillabaisse. Yet it is only fairly recently that American chefs have carved out a whole new area of fish cookery, serving up shellfish with beans and thick fillets of salmon and firm-textured white fish in aromatic light broths, paired with vegetables that range from delicate leeks and mushrooms to hearty turnips and cabbage.

Seafood stews are by and large easy to execute and quick-cooking, but they involve a little logistical planning, since most must be served as soon as they are ready. A way around this is to prepare the stew base ahead of time, have all the fish and shellfish prepped, and only at the last moment combine the two and cook the seafood.

Cod, halibut, and swordfish are three of my favorite fish for stewing, because they all have a fresh, clean taste and a meaty texture; cut into good-sized chunks, they hold together well during simmering. Almost any other firm white fish can be substituted; just be sure the thickness is close to that called for in the recipes. Thin fillets of sole are

invariably disappointing when cooked in this fashion, because no mat-
ter how careful you are, they flake apart.

     Shrimp and scallops are lovely easy additions to seafood
stew. Remember, however, that they cook in a mere two or three min-
utes. Overcooking will cause them to toughen and shrink, sometimes
appreciably, especially if they have been frozen. Clams and mussels
offer both their delicious meat and their juices, which can be an
important part of the stew base. And if you feel like splurging, nothing
creates a better seafood stew than lobster.

     Most of the fish and shellfish stews in this collection need
only some crusty grilled bread, rubbed with a raw garlic clove and
brushed lightly with a fruity olive oil, to make a lovely meal. Many,
such as the Ragout of Swordfish or the Thai-Style Crab and Fish Stew,
could be served either as a fish course to begin with or as the star of the
meal. Some, like the Scallop Pie and the Shrimp Curry with Mango
and Pineapple, are marvelous dishes for entertaining, and work very
well on a buffet. Both lobster stews, the classic Lobster à l'Armoricaine
and the Lobster Stewed in Whiskey Cream with Grilled Portobello
Mushrooms and Asparagus, are knockouts for your most elegant dinner
parties.

Lobster Stewed in Whiskey Cream with Grilled Portobello Mushrooms and Asparagus

4 to 6 Servings   *This is a drop-dead recipe that's as rich and intense-tasting as it is colorful and elegant. The entire recipe can be made in advance through Step 5, or you can finish it and reheat it the next day if you are very careful not to overcook the lobster. Serve as a first course or as the centerpiece of a very special dinner party.*

Because I cannot bear to hack up a live lobster, and the closest fish market is too far from my house to have them cut it up, I give instructions for blanching the lobster before beginning the recipe proper. If you are a more stalwart cook than I, begin with the cutting up of the lobster, of course, severing the spinal cord first.

> *2 live lobsters (1¼ to 1½ pounds each)*
> *¾ cup finely chopped shallots*
> *2 cups heavy cream*
> *⅔ cup dry vermouth*
> *3 tablespoons Scotch whiskey*
> *Dash of cayenne*
> *12 ounces thickly sliced portobello mushrooms*
> *2 teaspoons olive oil*
> *5 to 6 ounces asparagus, cut into 2-inch lengths, or sugar snap*
>   *peas, trimmed and cut diagonally in half if large*
> *2 tablespoons minced fresh chervil or parsley*

1. Preheat the oven to 425 degrees F.

2. Bring a large pot of water to a boil over high heat. Plunge the lobsters in headfirst and cook just for 2 to 3 minutes, until the tails are curled and the lobsters are dead. Immediately remove with tongs and rinse under cold running water. Using a cleaver or kitchen shears on a cutting board with a lip to catch the juices, cut the lobsters down the belly and scoop out and reserve any coral, which will appear black at this time. Discard the tomalley or reserve for another use.

Remove and discard the sand sack from the head. Remove the meat from the shells, reserving all the juices that run out of the lobsters. Cut the lobster meat into 1½- to 2-inch chunks. Cover and refrigerate the lobster meat and coral and juices separately.

3. Place the lobster shells in a roasting pan and set in the oven for 25 to 30 minutes, or until they are bright red and lightly browned. Break the roasted lobster shells into pieces and place in a large pot. Add 6 cups of water, cover, and boil over moderate heat for 30 minutes. Uncover and boil over high heat for 15 minutes longer. Strain through a fine sieve, return the lobster stock to a clean saucepan, and boil over high heat until reduced to 1½ cups, about 20 minutes.

4. Meanwhile, in a large saucepan, combine the shallots, cream, and vermouth. Boil over moderately low heat, stirring occasionally, until the liquid is reduced by half, about 20 minutes. Stir in the whiskey and cayenne; simmer for 3 minutes. Add the roasted lobster stock.

5. While the cream and stock are reducing, brush the mushrooms with the olive oil and grill over a hot fire in a barbecue grill or on a cast-iron grill pan, turning, until tender and nicely browned, about 7 minutes. Remove to a plate. In a large saucepan of boiling water, cook the asparagus until tender but still bright green, 2 to 3 minutes. Drain and rinse briefly under cold running water. Drain well. (The mushrooms and asparagus can be cooked several hours in advance and set aside at room temperature.)

6. Add the lobster meat, coral, and any remaining juices to the sauce and simmer 10 minutes, or until the lobster is opaque throughout and tender but still moist. Add the grilled mushrooms, along with any juices that have collected on the plate, and the asparagus. Ladle into soup plates and garnish with the chervil.

➤ All the elements for this stew can be prepared several hours in advance. The lobster base can even be made a day ahead. Once it is all assembled, though, it is best served immediately. I must admit, however, that I have reheated leftovers very successfully the next day, being careful to warm it gently, so the lobster does not toughen. I would not freeze this stew.

Lobster à l'Armoricaine

4 to 6 Servings

This is a lush recipe, which stretches two lobsters into enough richly flavored stew to feed six people. Serve in soup plates over a mound of steamed white rice. I like to begin with a simple plate of roasted asparagus or asparagus vinaigrette and finish with cheese and salad and a strawberry dessert.

> 2 live lobsters (1¼ pound each) preferably female
> 2 tablespoons olive oil
> ¼ cup Armagnac
> 5 tablespoons unsalted butter
> 4 shallots, minced
> ¾ pound tomatoes, peeled, seeded, and chopped
> 1 cup dry white wine
> 1½ tablespoons minced fresh tarragon or ¾ teaspoon dried
> ¼ teaspoon cayenne
> 1 tablespoon flour
> 1 tablespoon minced fresh chives or parsley

1. Either sever the lobsters' spinal cord and then proceed to Step 2 or, if you are squeamish like me, bring a large pot of water to a boil over high heat. Plunge the lobsters in headfirst and cook just for a minute or two, until the tails are curled and the lobsters are dead. Immediately remove with tongs and rinse under cold running water.

2. On a cutting board with a lip, using a cleaver or kitchen shears, cut the lobsters down the belly and scoop out and reserve all the green tomalley and any coral, which may appear black at this time. Remove and discard the sand sack. Cut up the edible parts of the lobsters into about 10 pieces roughly 2 inches large. Crack the shells. Reserve all the juices that run out of the lobsters. Coarsely chop up the shells from the head and put in a saucepan with 2 cups water. Boil over high heat until reduced by half, about 20 minutes; strain.

3. Meanwhile, in a large flameproof casserole, heat the oil over moderately high heat. Add the lobster pieces and sauté, turning, until the shells are bright red, 2 to 3 minutes. Reduce the heat to moderately low, add the Armagnac, avert

your face, and carefully ignite with a match. As soon as the flames subside, pour the lobster pieces and pan juices into a bowl.

4. In the same pan, melt 2 tablespoons of the butter over moderate heat. Add the shallots and cook until softened, about 2 minutes. Add the tomatoes and cook until they begin to form a sauce, 3 to 5 minutes. Pour in the wine and boil for 2 minutes. Add the lobster shell stock. Return the lobster pieces to the pan, along with any juices in the bowl and any other juices you collected when you cut up the lobsters. Add 1 tablespoon of the fresh tarragon (or all the dried) and the cayenne. Bring to a boil, reduce the heat to moderately low, and simmer, partially covered, 12 minutes. (The recipe can be prepared in advance to this point. If you do so, simmer for only 10 minutes, so the lobster does not overcook. Set aside, covered, for up to 1 hour at room temperature, or refrigerate for several hours. Reheat before proceeding.)

5. Mash the tomalley and coral with the remaining butter and the flour. Stir into the sauce and boil, stirring, until slightly thickened and smooth, about 2 minutes. Serve garnished with the remaining fresh tarragon and the chives.

➤ I have never tried to freeze this stew, and it is best freshly made, but it does reheat well the next day. Just be sure to warm over gentle heat so the lobster does not toughen.

Ragout of Mussels with Fennel and Mushrooms

4 to 6 Servings T*his recipe was inspired by Joel Robouchon's fabulous version of* mouclade *in Patricia Wells's* Simply French. *Big chunks of fennel and mushrooms turn this from a light first course into a substantial main-course stew. The trick is to brown the fennel first to bring out the nuttiness in its flavor. French Garlic Toasts (recipe follows) are the perfect accompaniment.*

> *2 large fennel bulbs*
>
> *3 tablespoons extra-virgin olive oil*
>
> *2 tablespoons unsalted butter*
>
> *2 medium leeks, halved lengthwise, then cut crosswise into*
>   *½-inch pieces*
>
> *12 ounces medium mushrooms, quartered*
>
> *1 teaspoon dried thyme leaves*
>
> *½ teaspoon salt*
>
> *⅛ teaspoon cayenne*
>
> *1½ tablespoons fresh lemon juice*
>
> *4 pounds mussels*
>
> *2 cups dry white wine*
>
> *2 large shallots, finely chopped*
>
> *½ cup chopped parsley*
>
> *Pinch of saffron threads*
>
> *½ cup heavy cream*
>
> *1 teaspoon cornstarch*

1. Trim the fennel bulbs. Cut them lengthwise in half and then cut each half into ½-inch wedges, cutting through a bit of the root with each wedge so that they hold together. In a large skillet, heat 2 tablespoons of the olive oil over high heat. Add half of the fennel wedges and sauté, turning, until nicely browned, 2 to 3 minutes on each side. With tongs, remove to a bowl and brown the remaining fennel in the same way. There should be enough oil left in the pan for both batches; if not, add a little more.

2. Melt 1 tablespoon of butter in the remaining 1 tablespoon olive oil in the same skillet over moderately high heat. Add the leeks and cook for about 2 minutes, until they begin to soften. Add the mushrooms and cook, stirring occasionally, until the leeks are soft and the mushrooms are beginning to brown, about 3 minutes. Season with ½ teaspoon of the thyme, the salt, and the lemon juice. Add ½ cup water to the skillet and bring to a boil, stirring with a wooden spoon to scrape up any browned bits from the bottom of the pan.

3 Return the fennel to the pan and gently mix with the mushrooms and leeks. Reduce the heat to moderately low, cover, and cook, turning the mixture once or twice, until the fennel is just tender, 5 to 7 minutes. Remove and set aside.

4. No more than an hour and a half before serving, scrub and debeard the mussels.

5. In a large covered flameproof casserole or stockpot, cook the shallots in the remaining 1 tablespoon butter over moderately high heat until softened, 1 to 2 minutes. Pour in the wine and bring to a boil. Add the remaining ½ teaspoon thyme, the cayenne, and ¼ cup of the chopped parsley. Add the mussels, cover the pot, and cook over high heat until they open, 3 to 5 minutes.

6. Remove the mussels to a large, wide serving bowl and cover to keep warm. Discard any that do not open. Strain the liquid in the pot through a fine mesh sieve or a double thickness of cheesecloth into a medium skillet or large saucepan. Crumble the saffron into the broth and boil over high heat until reduced by at least one third, about 3 minutes. Add the cream and boil 2 minutes longer. Meanwhile, reheat the fennel and mushrooms.

7. Dissolve the cornstarch in 2 tablespoons water. Stir into the mussel broth and boil, stirring until slightly thickened, 1 to 2 minutes. Taste and season with additional salt if needed. Pour the fennel-mushroom mixture over the mussels and fold gently to mix. Pour the sauce over all, sprinkle the remaining chopped parsley on top, and serve at once.

➤ This stew can be prepared through Step 3 up to several hours in advance. However, once it is finished, it should be served immediately, and it does not reheat or freeze well.

French Garlic Toasts

Makes 12 Y*ou'll find this has a very different effect than that of the kind of buttery garlic bread associated with Italian American restaurants. These toasts are simpler and somewhat more sophisticated, but no less garlicky, since what is used here is raw.*

12 slices of French bread, cut ½ inch thick
2 or 3 garlic cloves, cut in half
1 to ½ tablespoons extra-virgin olive oil

1. Toast the bread on both sides, either over a barbecue grill, under a broiler, or in a toaster.

2. Rub 1 side of each toast slice with the cut side of the garlic clove, changing pieces of garlic every several slices. (The hard toast grates a little of the raw garlic onto the bread.)

3. Brush a little olive oil over each slice. Serve at once.

Towny's Oyster Stew

4 Servings

Philippe Townsend Montant has been in the restaurant business most of his life. This is his tried and true recipe for a great classic. Because of its richness, this is best offered as a lunch or light supper, though it could serve as a very substantial starter. Accompany with pilot crackers and coleslaw on the side.

4 tablespoons clarified butter
½ cup finely diced celery
½ cup finely chopped onion
½ teaspoon Worcestershire sauce
¼ teaspoon Tabasco sauce
¼ teaspoon celery salt
2 dozen medium oysters, shucked, liquor reserved
3½ cups clam juice
1 cup medium-dry sherry
2 cups half-and-half
Freshly ground black pepper

1. In a large heavy saucepan, heat the butter over moderate heat. Add the celery and onion and cook until softened but not browned, 3 to 5 minutes.

2. Add the Worcestershire, Tabasco, celery salt, oysters with their liquor, clam juice, sherry, and half-and-half. Cook, stirring occasionally, until hot, but do not let boil, 4 to 5 minutes.

3. Season with pepper to taste. Serve at once.

➤ This stew should be served as soon as it is made. It does not reheat or freeze well.

Salmon-Corn Chowder

6 Servings

You could quibble about whether this substantial, chunky and thick chowder, bolstered with potatoes and corn, is really a stew or a soup. I like it for lunch or supper, with a side of coleslaw and in season a ripe tomato salad.

1¼ pounds salmon fillet
Salt
Freshly ground black pepper
4 large ears of sweet corn
2 tablespoons butter
¼ pound lean salt pork or thick-sliced bacon, cut into
    ¼-inch dice
2 medium onions, cut into ½-inch dice
¾ cup dry white wine
1 cup canned or bottled clam juice
2 cups whole, lowfat, or skim milk
1½ teaspoons minced fresh savory or ½ teaspoon dried
⅛ teaspoon cayenne
4 medium red potatoes, peeled and cut into ¾-inch dice
1 cup heavy cream
¼ cup minced fresh chives

1. Remove the skin from the salmon, pick out any small bones, and cut the fish into 1-inch pieces. Season lightly with salt and pepper. Cover and refrigerate while you prepare the chowder base.

2. Cut the kernels off 3 ears of corn. Grate the corn from the fourth ear on the large holes of a hand grater. Set all the corn aside.

3. In a large flameproof casserole, melt the butter over moderate heat. Add the salt pork and cook, stirring occasionally, until lightly browned, about 6 minutes. Remove with a slotted spoon and set aside. Add the onions to the pan and cook, stirring occasionally, until golden, 5 to 7 minutes.

4. Pour in the wine and boil over high heat until reduced by half, about 3 minutes. Add the clam juice, milk, savory, and cayenne and bring to a boil.

Add the potatoes, reduce the heat to moderate, and cook 8 minutes. Add the corn and cream and cook 3 to 5 minutes longer, until the corn is almost tender but still slightly crunchy.

5. Add the salmon and salt pork and simmer until the fish is just opaque throughout, 5 to 7 minutes. Stir 2 tablespoons of the chives into the chowder. Serve at once, with the remaining chives sprinkled on top.

➤ If you are careful not to overcook the salmon, this stew can be reheated the next day. I do not freeze it.

Scallop Pie with Sage Cream Crust

6 to 8 Servings

*S*uch easy-to-come-by specialty ingredients as buttery Yukon gold potatoes and Vidalia onions in season really make a difference in this savory potpie. For easier entertaining, prepare the entire dish through Step 4 and refrigerate. Bake just before serving, allowing an extra 5 to 10 minutes in the oven to allow it to come to temperature.

1½ cups clam juice

1½ cups half-and-half

1 pound Vidalia or other very sweet onions, cut into ½-inch dice

1 pound Yukon gold potatoes (3 medium), peeled and cut into
  ½-inch dice

½ teaspoon minced fresh sage or crumbled dry leaves

½ teaspoon dried thyme leaves

½ teaspoon salt

⅛ teaspoon cayenne

4 ears of fresh corn or 2 cups frozen or canned corn kernels

1¼ pounds bay or calico scallops, or sea scallops, cut into
  ½-inch dice

1 small red bell pepper, cut into ⅜-inch dice

2 teaspoons fresh lemon juice

2 tablespoons chopped parsley

2 tablespoons minced fresh chives

Sage Cream Crust (recipe follows)

1. Preheat the oven to 400 degrees F.

2. In a large nonreactive pot, combine the clam juice and half-and-half. Bring to a boil. Add the onions, potatoes, sage, thyme, salt, and cayenne. Partially cover and cook over moderate heat until the onions and potatoes are just barely tender, about 10 minutes.

3. Meanwhile, if using fresh corn, cut the kernels off 3 ears of corn and with the back of the knife, scrape the corn "cream" from the cobs. Using the

coarse holes of a hand grater, grate the remaining ear of corn. Stir all the corn into the pot. Bring to a boil, simmer 2 minutes, and remove from the heat. Let cool for 15 minutes, stirring occasionally.

4. Add the scallops, bell pepper, lemon juice, parsley, and chives and turn into a shallow 2½- to 3-quart casserole. Set the sage cream crust over the scallop casserole and trim the edge to 1 inch. Fold over and crimp the edge. Cut several steam vents in the pastry.

5. Bake 30 to 35 minutes, or until the crust is just beginning to brown. Serve at once.

➤ As mentioned in the headnote, this stew goes well from refrigerator to oven, when made several hours in advance. For informal dining, I have reheated leftovers the next day, and they taste very good, though the crust tends to get soggy. I do not freeze this potpie.

Sage Cream Crust

Makes a large single crust

> 2 cups all-purpose flour
>
> 1¼ teaspoons salt
>
> 1 teaspoon chopped fresh sage or ½ teaspoon dried
>
> ¼ teaspoon baking powder
>
> ⅛ teaspoon cayenne
>
> 6 tablespoons cold butter, cut into tablespoons
>
> ¼ cup vegetable shortening
>
> ⅓ to ½ cup heavy cream

1. Place the flour, salt, sage, baking powder, and cayenne in a food processor and whirl to blend. Add the butter and shortening and pulse 8 to 10 times, until the butter is the size of large peas.

2. Turn on the machine and immediately add ⅓ cup cream through the feed tube. Process only until the dough is evenly moistened. Do not let it ball on the blade or it will be overprocessed. If the dough appears too dry, add a little more cream 1 tablespoon at a time. Gather the pastry into a ball, flatten into a thick disk, wrap well, and refrigerate for at least 30 minutes.

3. Turn out onto a floured work surface or between sheets of floured plastic wrap and roll out dough into an oval or rectangle, depending on your dish, about ¼ inch thick.

Thai-Style Crab and Fish Stew with Cilantro and Lime

4 to 6 Servings   Tart and spicy, this bright, light stew is perfect as a first course or light lunch or supper. Thai fish sauce, called nuac nam, is now available in the Asian food sections of many supermarkets.

¾ pound firm-textured white fish fillets, such as snapper or bass
½ pound lump crabmeat
5 to 6 ounces shiitake mushrooms, stemmed
2 cups Rich Chicken Stock (page 232) or 1 cup reduced-sodium
    canned broth mixed with 1 cup water
1 tablespoon Thai fish sauce
1½ teaspoons minced fresh ginger
1 large garlic clove, crushed through a press
¼ teaspoon salt
3 medium carrots, peeled and cut into long, thin shreds
3 fresh mild long green chiles, seeded and thinly sliced
2 fresh hot red chiles, seeded and very thinly sliced
¾ pound Napa or celery cabbage, cut into 2-inch pieces
2 tablespoons fresh lime juice
2 scallions, thinly sliced
2 tablespoons coarsely chopped cilantro

1. Cut the fish fillets into 2- to 3-inch pieces. Pick over the crabmeat to remove any bits of shell or cartilage. Cover and refrigerate the seafood until time to cook. Cut the shiitake caps into 3 wedges each and set aside.

2. In a large flameproof casserole, combine the chicken stock, fish sauce, ginger, garlic, salt, and 2 cups of water. Bring to a boil. Reduce the heat to a simmer. Add the shiitake caps, carrots, green and red chiles, and cabbage. Simmer, uncovered, until just tender, 3 to 5 minutes.

3. Add the fish and crab. Simmer 3 minutes, or until the fish just begins to flake. Stir in the lime juice, scallions, and cilantro and serve at once.

➤ This delicate stew should be served as soon it is made. I do not reheat or freeze it.

Mediterranean Seafood Stew with Fennel, Tomatoes, and Olives

6 Servings

This is a fresh-tasting seafood stew that is light and quick and easy. It can be embellished with clams and/or mussels if you wish, but they are not necessary and are more work than the fish, scallops, and shrimp called for here. The chipotle chile adds just a hint of smokiness along with a touch of heat, which lends a deeper complexity to the simple sauce, flavored with fresh tomatoes, fresh and dried fennel, olives, and a pinch of saffron.

> *3 tablespoons extra-virgin olive oil*
> *2 medium leeks (white and tender green), chopped*
> *1 small fennel bulb (about ¾ pound), cut into thin slivers*
> *3 garlic cloves, chopped*
> *½ teaspoon fennel seeds, lightly crushed*
> *Pinch of saffron threads*
> *1½ pounds ripe tomatoes, peeled, seeded, and coarsely chopped*
> *1 dried chipotle chile or other dried hot pepper, broken in half*
> *¼ teaspoon salt*
> *1¾ cups dry white wine*
> *½ cup slivered Kalamata olives*
> *1 pound fresh halibut steaks, cut 1 inch thick*
> *1 pound fresh cod fillets*
> *½ pound scallops*
> *½ pound shrimp*
> *1 tablespoon chopped fresh chervil or parsley*

1. In a paella pan or very large nonreactive skillet, heat the olive oil over moderately high heat. Add the leeks and fennel and cook, stirring occasionally, until the vegetables are soft and the leeks are just beginning to color, about 7 minutes. Add the garlic and cook until fragrant, about 1 minute. Add the fennel seeds, saffron, tomatoes, chipotle chile, and salt. Cover and boil until the tomatoes begin to soften, 3 to 5 minutes. Pour in the wine and ¼ cup water and boil

3 minutes longer. Stir in the olives and set the sauce aside, covered, at room temperature. (The recipe can be prepared ahead to this point up, covered snugly, and set aside at room temperature for up to 3 hours or refrigerated for up to a day.)

2. Cut each type of fish into 6 chunks. Rinse the scallops, pat dry, and pull off the tough membrane from the side if you wish. Shell and devein the shrimp, leaving the tail shells intact for appearance. If you do this ahead, place the seafood in a bowl, cover with plastic wrap directly on the surface, and refrigerate for up to 6 hours until you are ready to cook it.

3. Reheat the sauce if necessary. Add the fish chunks and arrange the scallops and shrimp around them. Cover and simmer 5 minutes. Gently turn the chunks of fish over with a spatula and simmer until all the seafood is cooked through, about 5 minutes longer. Sprinkle the chervil on top and serve at once.

➤ While elements of this stew can be prepared several hours and up to a day in advance, as noted in the recipe, once finished, it should be served immediately. I do not reheat or freeze this dish.

Ragout of Seafood with Pesto and Plum Tomatoes

6 to 8 Servings

As a first course, all this vibrant stew needs is some crusty bread to sop up the generous amount of savory juices. As a main dish, you might want to ladle it over a bowl of linguine.

1 pound mussels

2 dozen littleneck clams

1½ tablespoons olive oil

2 shallots, minced

1 pound fresh plum tomatoes, peeled, seeded, and chopped,
*   or 1 can (14-ounce) Italian-style peeled tomatoes,*
*   drained and chopped*

1½ cups dry white wine

Dash of cayenne

1 pound shrimp

1 pound swordfish or halibut steak, cut into 1½-inch chunks

¼ cup Simple Pesto (page 214) or prepared pesto sauce with basil

¼ cup coarsely chopped fresh basil or parsley

1. Scrub and debeard the mussels. In a large saucepan, bring 1 cup water to a boil. Add the mussels and steam over high heat until they just open, 2 to 3 minutes. Remove the mussels to a bowl; discard any that do not open. Strain the liquid and reserve 1 cup.

2. Scrub the clams with a vegetable brush and set aside.

3. In a large flameproof casserole, heat the olive oil over moderate heat. Add the shallots and cook until softened, about 2 minutes. Add tomatoes and cook, stirring, until they turn into a chunky sauce, 3 to 5 minutes.

4. Add the wine, cayenne, and reserved mussel broth and bring to a boil. Add the clams, cover, and cook until they open, 7 to 10 minutes. (Discard any clams that do not open.) With a slotted spoon, remove the clams to a large serving dish and cover to keep warm. Add the shrimp and fish to the sauce and simmer until just opaque throughout, about 3 minutes. Remove to the dish with the clams.

5. Stir the pesto into the sauce in the pan. Add the mussels and stir them gently for a few seconds to reheat. Pour the sauce and mussels over the seafood and garnish with the chopped basil.

➤ Shellfish in general does not reheat or freeze well. This stew should be served as soon as it is made.

Shellfish Fra Diavolo

4 Servings T*his tasty dish wants plenty of crusty Italian bread for mopping up the spicy sauce. Once you make the easy base, you can really throw in any mix of shellfish you like best. Just be sure not to overcook them, or they will shrink and toughen.*

The lobster is an optional ingredient. If you omit it, the recipe will still serve 4; to serve 6, increase the shrimp and scallops to ¾ pound each.

1 pound mussels, scrubbed and debearded

3 to 4 tablespoons extra-virgin olive oil

½ pound shrimp, shelled and deveined

½ pound scallops

1 lobster (about 1¼ pounds), cut into 2-inch chunks (optional)

2 shallots, minced

2 garlic cloves, minced

1 cup dry white wine

1 (28-ounce) can crushed tomatoes

1 teaspoon dried oregano

½ teaspoon crushed hot red pepper

Pinch of sugar

2 dozen littleneck clams

2 tablespoons chopped parsley

1. In a large saucepan, steam the mussels in 1 cup boiling water until they just open, 2 to 3 minutes. Remove and set aside (discard any mussels that do not open). Discard the liquid or reserve for another use.

2. In a large flameproof casserole, heat 2 tablespoons of the oil over moderately high heat. Add the shrimp and scallops and cook, tossing, 2 minutes, or until nicely seared outside and just barely cooked through. With a slotted spoon, remove to a bowl. If using lobster, add another tablespoon olive oil to pan, add the lobster pieces and cook, turning, until the shell is bright red and the lobster is cooked about halfway, about 5 minutes. Remove to a separate bowl.

3. Reduce the heat to moderately low. Add the remaining 1 tablespoon olive oil, the shallots, and the garlic to the casserole and cook until softened,

about 2 minutes. Add the wine and boil until reduced by half, about 3 minutes. Add the crushed tomatoes, oregano, hot pepper, and sugar. Bring to a boil, reduce the heat and simmer, partially covered, 20 minutes.

4. Add the clams, cover, and cook over moderately high heat until they open, 7 to 10 minutes. With a large skimmer or slotted spoon, transfer the clams to a deep serving dish or bowl (discard any clams that do not open). Cover to keep warm. Add the optional lobster to the sauce and simmer 5 minutes, or until just opaque throughout. Add to the bowl with the clams. Add the mussels, shrimp, and scallops along with any juices that have collected in the bowls to the pan and turn them gently in the hot sauce to reheat. Immediately pour over the clams. Garnish with the parsley and serve at once.

➤ This stew should be served as soon as it is made. It does not reheat or freeze well.

Shrimp Curry with Mango and Pineapple

4 to 6 Servings

E*xotic fruits are easier and easier to come by in the produce section of supermarkets, and their sweet-tart flavors pair beautifully with the mild sweetness of shrimp. For a dinner, I usually try to find jumbo shrimp or tiger prawns. For a buffet, you'll get more shrimp per spoonful with ordinary extra-large shrimp. Serve with steamed rice.*

1¼ pounds shrimp in the shell
1 small onion, quartered
3 large stems of parsley
½ teaspoon black peppercorns
3 tablespoons olive oil
1 large white onion, cut into 1-inch squares
1 red bell pepper, cut into 1-inch squares
1 green bell pepper, cut into 1-inch squares
2 garlic cloves, chopped
1 fresh hot chile (red or green), seeded and minced
1½ tablespoons Madras curry powder
1 teaspoon ground coriander
½ teaspoon ground cumin
1 cup unsweetened coconut milk
1 tablespoon lime juice
½ teaspoon salt
1 mango, cut into large dice
½ small pineapple, cut into 1-inch dice (about 2 cups)

1. Shell and devein the shrimp, reserving the shells. Place the shells in a large saucepan with the quartered onion, parsley, and peppercorns. Add 4 cups water, or enough to cover by at least an inch, and bring to a boil. Boil, uncovered, 20 minutes. Strain the stock; there should be 1½ to 2 cups. Boil until reduced to 1 cup.

2. In a large flameproof casserole, heat the oil over moderately high heat. Add the white onion and the red and green bell peppers and sauté, stirring often, until the vegetables are slightly softened, about 5 minutes. Add the garlic, chile, curry powder, coriander, and cumin and cook, stirring, 1 to 2 minutes. Pour in the shrimp stock, coconut milk, lime juice, and salt. Bring to a boil, reduce the heat to moderate, and simmer, uncovered, 3 minutes.

3. Add the shrimp and simmer until just pink and loosely curled, about 2 minutes. Add the mango and pineapple, simmer 1 minute longer, and serve.

➤ This dish can be prepared through Step 2 several hours in advance, but once finished, it should be served immediately. Leftovers can be reheated gently the next day, but they will not be as good.

Shrimp and Sausage Gumbo

6 to 8 Servings

Whether you consider gumbo a stew or a soup, it is eaten in a bowl over a mound of steamed white rice, and there's no argument that its zippy flavor and offbeat character make it a great party dish. This recipe doubles easily, though you should add another 10 or 15 minutes to the cooking time of the vegetables base to allow for the greater volume. Further embellish, if you wish, with crabmeat or even chunks of leftover grilled chicken. While this recipe aims to be spicy, such is the incendiary nature of a good gumbo that a bottle of hot sauce on the table is a must.

¼ cup plus 2 tablespoons vegetable oil

½ pound smoked ham, cut into ½-inch dice

½ pound andouille or spicy smoked kielbasa, sliced

1 pound medium shrimp, shelled and deveined, shells reserved

1 cup dry white wine

2 bay leaves

3 large sprigs of parsley plus ⅓ cup chopped parsley

¼ cup all-purpose flour

2 onions, chopped

2 celery ribs with leafy tops, thinly sliced

4 garlic cloves, finely chopped

1 pound okra, thinly sliced

1½ pounds plum tomatoes, peeled and coarsely chopped or
    1 (28-ounce) can Italian-style peeled tomatoes, drained
    and chopped

1 green bell pepper, chopped

1 red bell pepper, chopped

1 teaspoon salt

1 teaspoon dried oregano

¾ teaspoon dried thyme leaves

½ to ¾ teaspoon cayenne, to taste

2½ tablespoons fresh lemon juice

Tabasco sauce

1. In a medium saucepan, heat ¼ cup of the oil. Add the ham and sausage and cook over moderately high heat, stirring, until lightly browned, about 3 minutes. With a slotted spoon, remove the meats to a plate and set aside. Add the shrimp shells to the oil and cook over moderately high heat, stirring, until the shells are pink and beginning to brown lightly, about 3 minutes. Remove the oil from the heat. With a slotted spoon, pressing to extract as much oil as possible back into the pan, remove the shrimp shells to a large saucepan. Pour the wine over the shrimp shells and bring to a boil. Boil over high heat until the wine is reduced by half, about 3 minutes. Add 5½ cups of water, the bay leaves, and the parsley sprigs, bring to a boil, reduce the heat to moderate, and boil until the liquid is again reduced by half, about 20 minutes. Strain the shrimp stock and set aside.

2. Meanwhile, add the flour to the shrimp oil and set over moderately low heat. Cook, stirring constantly, until the flour turns light brown, 3 to 4 minutes. Immediately remove from the heat and continue to stir until the roux cools slightly. It will continue to cook and darken for a few minutes after you remove it from the heat, so do not overcook or it will burn. It should end up nut brown in color.

3. In a large flameproof casserole, heat the remaining 2 tablespoons oil. Add the onions and cook over moderately high heat, stirring occasionally, until they are golden and beginning to brown, 5 to 7 minutes. Add the celery and garlic and cook 2 minutes longer. Stir in the okra, tomatoes, bell peppers, salt, oregano, thyme, cayenne, and 1½ tablespoons of the lemon juice. Add 2 cups of the shrimp stock. Bring to a boil, reduce the heat to moderately low, cover, and simmer, stirring occasionally, 45 minutes.

4. Blend the remaining stock into the roux and stir into the gumbo. Add the reserved ham and sausage. Simmer 15 minutes. Add the shrimp and simmer 3 minutes, or until pink and curled. Stir in the remaining lemon juice and the chopped parsley. Season with additional salt and Tabasco sauce to taste.

➤ This stew reheats well for up to 3 days in the refrigerator, but the shrimp may toughen a bit. Stored in a tightly covered container, it can be frozen for up to 3 months.

Fish and Shellfish Stews

Ragout of Swordfish with Shiitake Mushrooms

4 Servings

A *contemporary blend of East and West highlights this stylish stew, which should be served in a soup plate, with crusty bread on the side. Begin with an artichoke or asparagus vinaigrette and allow yourself a dressy chocolate dessert.*

1½ pounds swordfish steak, cut about 1 inch thick

Salt

Freshly ground black pepper

½ pound shiitake mushrooms

3 large shallots, minced

¾ cup dry vermouth

⅔ cup heavy cream

2 whole star anise

1 stalk of lemongrass or a 1 by 3-inch strip of lemon zest

1 cup dry white wine, preferably Chardonnay

½ cup julienned carrot

½ cup julienned snow pea pods

1. Cut the swordfish into oblong chunks about 1½ by 4 inches. Season with salt and pepper and set aside.

2. Remove and discard the stems from the shiitakes. Thinly slice the caps on a slant, so the thin slices are as wide as possible.

3. In a large, deep skillet or flameproof casserole, bring the shallots, vermouth, cream, star anise, and lemongrass to a boil over moderately high heat. Boil until reduced by half, about 2 minutes. Add the wine and boil until reduced by half, about 3 minutes.

4. Add 1⅓ cups of water and ¼ teaspoon salt. Reduce the heat to moderately low and simmer 3 minutes. Add the swordfish, cover, and poach 3 minutes. Stir in the shiitakes and continue to cook until the fish is just barely opaque in the center, about 3 minutes longer.

5. With a wide spatula, divide the swordfish among 4 shallow soup plates. Add the carrot and snow peas to the stock in the pan and boil 1 to 2 minutes longer, until the vegetables are brightly colored and crisp-tender. Pour the sauce, shiitakes, and vegetables over the fish and serve at once.

➤ This stew is best served freshly made, though you can prepare the base through Step 3 hours in advance. Any leftovers can be stored overnight in the refrigerator, but reheat them gently. The stew can be frozen for up to 2 months.

Provençal Tuna Stew with Olives and Grilled Zucchini

6 Servings

T*una is so dark and sturdy that some people might think this is a meat stew. Serve with pasta, rice, or couscous.*

2 pounds tuna steak, cut about 1½ inches thick

3½ tablespoons extra-virgin olive oil

3 garlic cloves, 1 crushed, 2 minced

½ teaspoon dried oregano

2 teaspoons grated lemon zest

1 to 2 tablespoons fresh lemon juice

3 medium zucchini

1½ tablespoons drained tiny capers

1½ cups dry white wine

2 teaspoons tomato paste, preferably sun-dried

1 cup fish stock or ½ cup clam juice diluted with ½ cup water

Freshly ground pepper

½ cup Niçoise olives

2 tablespoons chopped parsley

1. Cut the tuna into 1½-inch chunks. Place it in a bowl and add 1½ tablespoons of the olive oil, the crushed garlic, oregano, 1 teaspoon of the lemon zest, and 1 tablespoon of the lemon juice. Toss to mix. Let marinate at room temperature 30 minutes.

2. Meanwhile, light a hot fire in a charcoal or gas grill. Trim the zucchini and split them in half lengthwise. Brush with 1½ teaspoons of the olive oil and grill, turning, until nicely browned and crisp-tender, about 5 to 7 minutes. Cut each half into 1½-inch lengths.

3. Remove the tuna from its marinade and pat dry; reserve any marinade in the bowl. In a large flameproof casserole, heat the remaining 1½ tablespoons olive oil over high heat. Add the tuna and sauté, turning, until the tuna is browned outside, but still rare inside, about 3 minutes. As the fish browns, remove it to a plate.

4. Add the minced garlic, capers, and any marinade remaining in the bowl to the pan and cook for 30 to 60 seconds. Pour in the wine and boil until reduced by about one-third, 2 to 3 minutes. Stir in the tomato paste until blended. Add the fish stock and remaining lemon zest and lemon juice.

5. Return the fish to the pan and simmer to the desired degree of doneness; I like it until just opaque throughout but still juicy, which takes about 3 minutes. Season with pepper to taste. Add the grilled zucchini and the olives, stir in the parsley, and serve at once.

➤ This stew is best freshly made. It can be reheated gently after several hours, but be careful, because the zucchini can turn mushy and the tuna dry and tough if they are overcooked. I do not recommend freezing this dish.

Vegetable and Bean Stews

Probably one of the most exciting new areas of cooking is the culinary exploration of vegetables. We know they're good for us, they are beautiful, and they possess a range of flavors and textures that's as broad as the plant kingdom. This chapter posed a real challenge to me, because although like so many people I've cut down on red meat and just naturally eat pasta or some other meatless dish for dinner at least a couple of nights a week, I am not a vegetarian, and deciding what makes a main dish of vegetables, with or without beans, was hard for me to determine at first.

But it didn't take much tasting to realize that a bowl of vegetables, cooked in a savory broth, punctuated perhaps with pungent garlic or the breezy zest of fresh ginger, enlivened with fragrant herbs and sweet or piquant spices, can be just as satisfying as a juicy grilled steak or roast loin of pork. The lighter of these recipes, Navarin of Spring Vegetables or Grilled Vegetable Ragout with Goat Cheese Garlic Toasts, would make a lovely first course or a light evening meal. The more substantial dishes, such as Smoky Vegetable Chili with Pinto Beans or the Greek Green Bean Stew with Squash and Potatoes, are

immensely satisfying meals in a bowl. Served in smaller portions, many of these can function as complex vegetable side dishes to a small serving of almost any grilled or roasted meat or chicken.

All the stews in this chapter are vegetarian in that, with the exception of one optional ham hock in the Rosemary Lentil Stew with Goat Cheese and Sun-Dried Tomatoes, there is no meat, chicken, or fish called for. In the recipes that are based on stock, I have listed my favorite for that particular dish first — sometimes vegetable stock, sometimes chicken stock. In all instances, one can be substituted for the other with minimal compromise in flavor. And occasionally, water is an acceptable substitute. Where canned broth works acceptably well, it is included as a choice. If I do not mention it, it means in that particular recipe, I feel the flavor of the stock is so prominent that the homemade version is a much better choice.

While freshness is the key to flavor in almost any food, with vegetables it is paramount; so choose your recipe according to seasonal availability and the quality in your market. Make sensible substitutions wherever you feel they are appropriate. I hope this chapter helps you to enjoy the rich variety of colors, flavors, and textures that vegetables and beans can add to our dining pleasure.

Easy Vegetarian Chili With Bulgur and Beans

6 to 8 Servings

I *like this substantial stew with a dollop of sour cream on top. Pass a bottle of hot sauce on the side.*

2 medium onions, chopped
2 celery ribs, chopped
¼ cup extra-virgin olive oil
6 garlic cloves, chopped
2½ tablespoons chili powder
½ teaspoon ground cinnamon
2 (14½-ounce) cans recipe-ready diced tomatoes, with their juice
2 cups Vegetable Stock (page 235) or chicken broth
2 carrots, peeled and coarsely chopped
1 small green bell pepper, chopped
1 pound cabbage (½ medium head), coarsely chopped
½ pound cauliflower, coarsely chopped (about 2 cups)
1 medium zucchini, coarsely chopped (about 2 cups)
¾ cup bulgur
1 (15-ounce) can dark red kidney beans, rinsed and drained
Salt

1. In a large flameproof casserole, cook the onions and celery in the olive oil, covered, over moderately low heat for 5 minutes. Uncover, raise the heat to moderate, and cook, stirring, until the onions are golden, about 8 minutes.

2. Add the garlic and cook 1 minute. Add the chili powder and cinnamon and cook, stirring, 1 minute longer. Pour in the tomatoes with their juice and the stock. Add 2 cups water. Bring to a boil. Add the carrots, bell pepper, cabbage, and cauliflower. Bring to a simmer, partially cover, and cook for 30 minutes, or until the cabbage is very soft.

3. Add the zucchini and bulgur, cover, and cook 10 minutes longer. Stir in the kidney beans and cook 5 minutes longer. Season with additional salt to taste.

➤ This stew can be refrigerated for up to 2 days. Do not freeze it.

Braised Bean Curd with Chinese Cabbage and Shiitake Mushrooms

4 to 5 Servings

With its licorice overtones of star anise and savory earthiness of shiitake mushrooms, this stew will convert even bean curd skeptics. Because cabbage becomes stronger upon standing, this stew is best eaten within several hours of being prepared. Served with rice, it makes quite a substantial vegetarian meal.

3 tablespoons sesame seeds

3½ cups Rich Chicken Stock (page 232) or Vegetable Stock (page 235)

5 scallions, 3 whole with roots trimmed, 2 sliced

3 slices of fresh ginger

3 garlic cloves, smashed

6 whole star anise pods

1 small hot dried red pepper

1 ounce dried shiitake mushrooms

2½ ounces bean thread noodles

2 tablespoons dry sherry

1 tablespoon dark soy sauce

1 large Chinese celery cabbage or Napa cabbage (2 pounds), cut crosswise into 1½- to 2-inch pieces

1 pound firm tofu or pressed Chinese bean curd, cut into ½-inch-thick slices

¼ teaspoon salt

1. In a dry medium skillet, toast the sesame seeds over moderate heat, shaking the pan often, until fragrant, 2 to 3 minutes. Remove to a plate and set aside.

2. In a large flameproof casserole, combine the stock, 3 whole scallions, ginger, garlic, star anise, and hot pepper. Bring to a simmer, reduce the heat to low, cover, and cook 20 minutes to blend the flavors. Strain the stock and return to the pan.

3. While the stock is simmering, place the shiitake mushrooms in a medium heatproof bowl and cover with 1½ cups boiling water. Let stand until soft, 15 to 20 minutes. Remove the mushrooms, squeezing the extra liquid back into bowl. Cut off the stems. Halve the caps if they are very large. Strain the mushroom soaking liquid and add to the stock.

4. Soak the bean thread noodles in a bowl of cold water until they are softened and pliable, 10 to 15 minutes. Drain and cut into 4-inch lengths.

5. Meanwhile, return the stock to a boil. Stir in the sherry and soy sauce Add the Chinese cabbage and the mushroom caps and simmer 5 minutes. Add the tofu slices and salt and simmer 5 minutes longer, or until the cabbage is just tender. Add the bean thread noodles and stir gently to mix them in. Ladle into bowls, sprinkle on the toasted sesame seeds and sliced scallions on top, and serve at once.

➤ As mentioned in the headnote, this stew should be eaten within several hours of being made. Leftovers can be reheated the next day, but the flavor will not be as good. I do not recommend freezing it.

Beet and Cabbage Stew with Potato–Blue Cheese Pirogi

8 to 10 Servings

This thick vegetarian borscht becomes a hearty meal when served with two or three pirogi.

3 cups Rich Chicken Stock (page 232) or Vegetable Stock
    (page 235) or water
1 (28-ounce) can Italian peeled tomatoes, coarsely chopped
2 medium leeks (white and tender green), cut into ½-inch slices
2 medium onions, chopped
1 tart apple, peeled and coarsely chopped
1 bay leaf
1 teaspoon ground coriander
2 cloves
1 teaspoon salt
½ teaspoon freshly ground black pepper
1 small head of green cabbage, cut into 1-inch chunks
2 pounds fresh beets, peeled and cut into 1-inch chunks
4 medium carrots, peeled and cut into 1- to 1½-inch lengths
3 red potatoes, peeled if desired and cut into 1½-inch chunks
¼ cup chopped fresh dill
2 tablespoons fresh lemon juice
Potato–Blue Cheese Pirogi (recipe follows)

1. In a large stockpot, combine the stock, tomatoes with their juices, leeks, onions, apple, bay leaf, coriander, cloves, salt, and pepper. Bring to a boil. Add the cabbage, and cook, stirring, until it begins to wilt, about 10 minutes.

2. Add the beets, carrots, potatoes, and 2 tablespoons of the chopped dill. Cover and cook over moderate heat 20 minutes. Uncover and boil slowly 20 to 30 minutes longer, until the vegetables are tender.

3. Stir in the lemon juice. To serve, add 2 or 3 pirogi to each bowl and sprinkle the remaining chopped dill on top.

➤ Before adding the pirogi, the stew can be refrigerated and reheated the next day. Do not freeze.

Potato–Blue Cheese Pirogi

Makes 24

1 egg
¾ teaspoon salt
1¾ cups flour
1 pound baking potatoes (2 medium), peeled and cut into
1½- to 2-inch chunks
4 tablespoons butter
1 small onion, minced
3 ounces cream cheese, softened
2 ounces Roquefort or other good blue cheese
Dash of cayenne

1. To make the dough: In a medium bowl, beat the egg with ½ cup water and ¼ teaspoon of the salt until blended. Stir in the flour. Knead with your hands in the bowl for a minute or two to mix well. The dough will be a bit sticky. Cover and set aside while you make the filling.

2. Bring a large saucepan of salted water to a boil. Boil the potatoes until very tender, about 15 minutes; drain.

3. Meanwhile, in a small skillet, melt 2 tablespoons of the butter over moderately high heat. Add the onion and cook, stirring often, until the onion is soft and golden brown, 6 to 8 minutes.

4. Pass the potatoes through a ricer or mash with a potato masher until smooth. Blend in the remaining butter, the cream cheese, Roquefort cheese, remaining ½ teaspoon salt, and cayenne. Scrape the onion and all the melted butter from the skillet into the potatoes and mix well.

5. For the pirogi, roll the dough into 2 ropes about 12 inches long. Cut each rope into 1-inch lengths and roll into a ball. Roll each piece into a 4-inch circle and fill with about 1 tablespoon of the potato filling. Moisten the edges with water, fold over into a half-moon shape, and press and pinch between your fingertips to seal.

6. In a large saucepan of boiling salted water, cook the pirogi until tender, 2 to 3 minutes. Remove with a skimmer and drain.

Smoky Vegetable Chili with Pinto Beans

6 to 8 Servings

This is a tasty and attractive chili, with its chunks of yellow squash, orange carrot, and red and green roasted peppers. A mild smokiness is imparted by both grilling some of the vegetables first and by the addition of dried chipotle chile, which is available in Mexican markets and in many supermarkets. Serve over brown rice, with tortilla chips and shredded Cheddar cheese on the side.

2 medium eggplant (1¼ pounds each)

1 red bell pepper

1 green bell pepper

3 tablespoons olive oil

2 medium onions, chopped

3 garlic cloves, chopped

2 tablespoons chili powder

2 teaspoons ground cumin

2 carrots, peeled and cut into ⅜-inch dice

1 large celery rib, chopped

2 yellow squash (about 1 pound), cut into ⅜-inch dice

1½ cups crushed tomatoes with added puree

1 (14½-ounce) can vegetable broth

1 or 2 dried chipotle chiles, to taste

1 teaspoon dried oregano

1 bay leaf

1 (15-ounce) can pinto beans, rinsed and drained

½ teaspoon salt

1. Light a hot fire in a barbecue grill. Grill the eggplant, turning, until they are soft and well blackened all over, 25 to 30 minutes. Remove the blackened skin and coarsely chop the eggplant. Grill the red and green peppers, turning, until charred, 10 to 15 minutes. Peel, seed, and cut into ⅜ inch dice.

2. In a large flameproof casserole, heat the olive oil over moderately high heat. Add the onions and cook, stirring, until lightly browned, about 8 minutes. Add the garlic and cook 1 minute. Add the chili powder and cumin and cook, stirring, 1 minute longer.

3. Stir in the carrots, celery, squash, and eggplant. Add the tomatoes with their liquid, the vegetable broth, chipotle chile, oregano, and bay leaf. Cover and simmer over low to moderately low heat 30 minutes, stirring occasionally to prevent the bottom from sticking.

4. Remove and discard the bay leaf and chile. Add the pinto beans, roasted peppers, and salt. Cover and simmer 5 minutes.

➤ This stew will reheat well after up to 2 days in the refrigerator. Because the texture is so important, I do not freeze it.

Grilled Corn and Tomatillo Stew with Rajas and Roasted Garlic

4 to 6 Servings P*oblano peppers, with their deep earthiness and mild to biting spiciness, provide the dominant note in this Mexican-flavored stew (rajas are thin strips of roasted peppers). If you add a couple of skinless, boneless chicken breasts cut into thick strips in Step 2, you will have a fabulous party dish feeding six to eight people. Serve with rice, tortillas, and an avocado and tomato salad.*

> *4 large ears of corn*
> *1 head of garlic*
> *¾ pound poblano peppers*
> *1 red bell pepper*
> *1 large white onion, thickly sliced into rings*
> *1½ tablespoons vegetable oil*
> *1 pound fresh tomatillos*
> *3 cups Rich Chicken Stock (page 232), Vegetable Stock*
>   *(page 235), or reduced-sodium canned broth*
> *1 tablespoon toasted cumin seeds (see* Note*)*
> *1 teaspoon salt*
> *1 cup shredded sharp Cheddar cheese, lightly packed*
> *¼ cup grated Romano cheese*
> *½ cup sour cream*
> *2 tablespoons chopped cilantro*

1. Light a fire in a charcoal or gas grill. Shuck the corn and cut off the top of the garlic head. Brush 2 corn ears, the garlic, poblanos, bell pepper, and onion rings with the oil. Wrap the garlic in foil, set on the grill away from the hottest part of the fire, and roast until tender, 40 to 45 minutes.

2. Meanwhile, grill the remaining corn, turning, until lightly browned, 12 to 15 minutes; the onion rings and tomatillos, turning the onion rings once and the tomatillos often, until browned, 5 to 8 minutes; and the poblanos and bell pepper until charred all over, 8 to 10 minutes. Remove the vegetables from the grill as they are done.

3. Cut the kernels from the roasted corn cobs. Cut the onion rings into quarters. Steam the peppers in a brown paper bag for 5 to 10 minutes, then peel, seed, and cut into thin strips. Squeeze the garlic from its skin. In a food processor, coarsely puree the roasted tomatillos with their skins and the garlic.

4. In a large flameproof casserole, bring the chicken stock to a boil. With the large holes of a hand grater, grate the corn from the remaining 2 ears. Add to the broth along with the toasted cumin seeds and salt. Boil 5 minutes. Add the tomatillo-garlic puree, reduce the heat slightly, and simmer 5 minutes longer. Add the grilled corn, peppers, and onion and simmer 2 minutes. Stir in the Cheddar and Romano cheese until melted. Stir in the sour cream and heat through. Serve garnished with chopped cilantro.

◇ **Note:** Toast cumin seeds in a small dry skillet over moderate heat, shaking the pan until they are lightly browned and fragrant, 2 to 3 minutes. Immediately transfer to a small bowl or plate to stop the cooking.

➤ Stored in a tightly closed container, this stew can be kept in the refrigerator for up to 3 days or in the freezer for up to 3 months.

Mary Earnshaw's Million-Dollar Corn Stew

4 to 6 Servings

*T*hough this is really a chowder, it is so thick and rich-tasting that the Earnshaw family calls it a stew. It's a recipe that comes from Mary Earnshaw, whose son Billy grows vast quantities of excellent corn. According to Mary, a family named McCage, traveling north from their winter home in Florida, stopped along the way for a bite to eat. The corn chowder they were served was so good that Mr. McCage went back for the recipe. The chef was reluctant, but Mr. McCage crossed his palm with a sum of money, which grows larger each year the story is told.

6 ears of fresh corn
8 tablespoons unsalted butter
⅓ cup flour
4 cups milk (2 percent is fine)
1 large onion, chopped
1 medium green bell pepper, chopped
2 large or 3 medium tomatoes, peeled, seeded, and chopped
Salt
Freshly ground black pepper

1. Grate the corn from the cob with an old-fashioned corn grater or use the large holes on a handheld grater. There should be about 2 cups.

2. In a medium saucepan, melt 6 tablespoons of the butter. Add the flour and cook over moderate heat, stirring, for 1 to 2 minutes without allowing the flour to color to make a roux. Whisk in the milk and bring to a boil, whisking until smooth and thickened, 1 to 2 minutes. Remove from the heat and set the white sauce aside.

3. In a large flameproof casserole or soup pot, melt the remaining 2 tablespoons of butter over moderate heat. Add the onion and cook 2 minutes. Add the pepper and cook until the onion is soft but not brown, 2 to 3 minutes longer. Add the tomatoes and cook, stirring occasionally, until they soften to a coarse puree, 3 to 5 minutes.

4. Stir the white sauce into the vegetables. Add the grated corn, partially cover, and simmer for 20 to 30 minutes, or until the stew is very thick. Season with salt and pepper to taste.

➤ Stored in a tightly closed container, this dish keeps well in the refrigerator for up to 3 days and in the freezer for up to 6 months.

Indian Chick-Pea and Potato Curry

3 to 4 Servings

*I*ti and Satya Arya, who own a *family-style Indian restaurant in Binghamton, New York, gave me this recipe. It is drier than many of our American stews. Serve as a main course with rice, Cucumber Raita (recipe follows), and a chutney, or as a side dish.*

2 medium red potatoes (¾ pound)

1 (16-ounce) can chick-peas (garbanzo beans)

3 garlic cloves, smashed

1½ inches fresh ginger, peeled

2 teaspoons ground coriander

2 teaspoons ground cumin

½ teaspoon amchoor (see Note)

½ teaspoon salt

½ teaspoon freshly ground black pepper

⅛ to ¼ teaspoon cayenne

2 tablespoons vegetable oil

1 small onion, thinly sliced

1 teaspoon whole cumin seeds

2 black cardamom pods

1 large tomato (½ pound), chopped

½ teaspoon sugar

¼ teaspoon garam masala

1 tablespoon chopped cilantro

1. In a medium saucepan of boiling water, cook the potatoes for 25 minutes, or until tender; drain. As soon as you can handle them, peel the potatoes and cut them into 1½-inch chunks. Place the potatoes in a medium bowl. Drain and rinse the chick-peas. Drain well and add to the potatoes.

2. Chop together the garlic and 1 inch of the ginger until finely minced. Add to the potatoes. In a small bowl, mix together the ground coriander, ground cumin, amchoor, salt, black pepper, and cayenne. Sprinkle over the potatoes and chick-peas and toss to mix. Set aside at room temperature for 30 to 60 minutes.

3. Cut the remaining ginger into very fine dice. In a wok or large skillet, heat the oil over moderate heat. Add the onion and cook, stirring, until golden brown, about 7 minutes. Add the cumin seeds and cook 30 seconds. Add the ginger and cardamom pods and cook 30 seconds longer. Add the tomato and cook, stirring often, until softened, about 2 minutes. Throw in the chick-peas and potatoes and toss. Add ½ cup water and the sugar and simmer 5 minutes. Transfer to a serving dish and sprinkle the garam masala and cilantro on top.

◇ **Note:** Amchoor is ground mango leaf and can be purchased in Indian or Asian markets. As a substitute, 1 tablespoon of tamarind paste can be added with the tomato. Or stir in 1 tablespoon lemon juice at the very end.

➤ This dish can be stored in the refrigerator for up to 2 days and reheated. If you do so, you may need to add a little more water. Warm over moderately low heat or in a microwave oven. I do not recommend freezing this stew.

Cucumber Raita

Makes about 3 cups

> *1 medium cucumber*
> *1 pint plain nonfat yogurt*
> *½ cup finely diced white onion*
> *½ teaspoon sugar*
> *⅛ teaspoon cayenne*

1. Peel the cucumber, cut lengthwise in half, and scoop out the seeds with a large spoon. Finely dice the cucumber.

2. In a medium bowl, combine the diced cucumber, yogurt, onion, sugar, and cayenne. Mix well. Serve at once or cover and refrigerate for up to 3 hours before serving.

Curried Vegetables with Chick-Peas and Raisins

6 Servings
Almost all vegetables take well to curry seasoning, and the addition of chick-peas and raisins, as well as yogurt, makes this an especially nutritious as well as delicious stew. Serve with rice and pass a bowl of yogurt or Cucumber Raita (see page 209).

2 medium onions, chopped

3 tablespoons vegetable oil

3 garlic cloves, minced

1 tablespoon finely chopped fresh ginger

1½ tablespoons ground coriander

1½ teaspoons ground cumin

½ teaspoon ground cinnamon

½ teaspoon cayenne

½ teaspoon turmeric

1 (14-ounce) can recipe-ready diced tomatoes, with their juices

1 bay leaf

½ medium green bell pepper, chopped

2 or 3 medium carrots, peeled and thickly sliced

½ pound cauliflower, broken into florets (2 cups)

1 small eggplant, peeled and cut into 1-inch dice

2 medium red potatoes, peeled and cut into 1-inch dice

1½ teaspoons salt

1 cup green beans, cut into 1-inch lengths

1 medium-large sweet potato, peeled and cut into 1-inch chunks

1 (16-ounce) can chick-peas (garbanzo beans)

Juice and chopped pulp from 1 large lemon

½ cup raisins

½ cup plain nonfat yogurt

1. In a large flameproof casserole, cook the onions in the oil over moderate heat, stirring occasionally, until golden and just beginning to brown, 5 to 7 minutes. Add the garlic, ginger, coriander, cumin, cinnamon, cayenne, and turmeric. Cook, stirring, 2 to 3 minutes, until the spices are toasted and fragrant and the garlic is softened.

2. Pour the tomatoes with their juices into the pan. Add the bay leaf, bell pepper, carrots, cauliflower, eggplant, red potatoes, salt, and 2 cups water. Bring to a simmer, cover, and cook over moderately low heat, stirring occasionally, until the vegetables are just tender, 20 to 25 minutes.

3. Meanwhile, in a medium saucepan of boiling water, cook the green beans until crisp-tender, 3 to 5 minutes. Drain, rinse under cold running water, and drain again.

4. Add the green beans, sweet potato, chick-peas, lemon juice and pulp, and raisins to the curry. Simmer 10 to 15 minutes longer, until all the vegetables are tender. Remove and discard the bay leaf. Stir in the yogurt, heat through, and serve.

➤ This dish can be reheated after up to 2 days in the refrigerator. I do not recommend freezing it.

Fall Vegetable Stew with Fresh Tomatoes, Corn, and Pesto

6 to 8 Servings

Some people might be able to enjoy this stew in August, but in much of the country corn and tomatoes really peak in September, and the fresh basil remains bushed out until the first frost. Add a little more water or stock, cut the vegetables into smaller pieces, and this tasty, healthful dish turns into a chowder. The secret ingredient is a dried chipotle chile, which adds a lovely touch of smokiness as well as heat. Brightly flavored with basil and garlic, and a sprinkling of good Parmesan cheese if you like, it makes a very satisfying meal in a bowl.

- *2½ to 3 pounds ripe red tomatoes*
- *2 tablespoons olive oil*
- *2 medium leeks (white and tender green) or onions, coarsely chopped*
- *3 garlic cloves, chopped*
- *1 dried chipotle chile*
- *2 teaspoons salt*
- *¾ teaspoon ground coriander*
- *¼ teaspoon freshly ground black pepper*
- *3 cups Rich Chicken Stock (page 232) or 2 cups reduced-sodium chicken broth plus 1 cup water, or 3 cups water*
- *3 medium carrots, peeled and cut crosswise on an angle into 1-inch pieces*
- *3 to 4 medium red or yellow potatoes, peeled and cut into 1-inch chunks*
- *½ medium cabbage (1 pound), very coarsely chopped*
- *4 ears of sweet corn*
- *2 medium zucchini, cut into 1-inch chunks*
- *Simple Pesto (recipe follows)*
- *Grated Parmesan cheese*

1. Peel the tomatoes either by holding them with tongs over the open flame of a gas stove or by dunking them for 10 to 30 seconds in a pot of boiling water. Peel the tomatoes and cut out the cores on top. Coarsely chop the tomatoes, but reserve all the juice and seeds as well as the pulp.

2. In a large soup pot, heat the oil over moderate heat. Add the leeks, cover, and cook 2 to 3 minutes, until they begin to wilt. Uncover and continue to cook, stirring occasionally, until they are soft and just beginning to take on some color, 3 to 5 minutes longer. Add the garlic and cook for 2 minutes.

3. Stir in the tomatoes with all their juices. Add the chipotle chile, salt, coriander, pepper, chicken stock, carrots, potatoes, and cabbage. If necessary, add a little more water to just cover the vegetables, but remember the cabbage will give off a fair amount of liquid. Bring to a boil, cover, and cook over moderately low heat, stirring occasionally, 25 minutes. Taste the broth after 15 minutes. If it is getting too spicy-hot for your taste, remove the chile. If it is fine, remove the chile after 25 minutes of cooking.

4. Meanwhile, cut the corn kernels off the cob and run the dull edge of the knife down the cobs to get all the "cream." Add all the corn and the zucchini to the soup and cook 10 minutes. Serve with separate bowls of the pesto and grated Parmesan cheese passed on the side.

➤ Stored in a tightly closed container in the refrigerator, this stew reheats well and tastes even better the next day. It should not, however, be frozen, because the carrots and potatoes will become mealy and the zucchini will lose its texture.

Simple Pesto

Makes about ½ cup

I call this pesto simple because all it contains are fresh basil, garlic, and your best extra-virgin olive oil—no nuts or cheese. It is simple to make as well—a moment in a food processor. Even though it is processed, I like to puree the garlic first to remove any lumps.

¼ cup fresh basil leaves
2 or 3 garlic cloves
⅓ cup extra-virgin olive oil
Salt
Freshly ground black pepper

1. Place the basil in a food processor. Squeeze the garlic cloves through a press into the processor. Turn on the machine and add the oil through the feed tube. Scrape down the sides of the bowl and process until the basil is finely chopped.

2. Scrape the pesto into a small bowl and season lightly with salt and pepper.

Garlicky Beans and Greens

4 to 6 Servings

T*his is a good vegetarian dish all by itself, or you could serve it over pasta, in which case it would be enough for 6 to 8 servings. While it looks like there is a mountain of the raw greens, once they are trimmed and cooked, they reduce in volume substantially.*

1 large bunch of kale (about 2 pounds)

1 large bunch of collards (1½ pounds)

6 garlic cloves, thinly sliced

3 tablespoons extra-virgin olive oil

4 cups Rich Chicken Stock (page 232), Vegetable Stock (page 235), or 1 (12¾-ounce) can reduced-sodium chicken broth diluted with 2 cups water

1 chipotle chile or other small dried hot pepper

2 cans (15 ounces each) Great Northern white beans, rinsed and drained

1½ tablespoons lemon juice

1 tablespoon cider vinegar

Salt

Freshly ground black pepper

1. Rinse the greens well and remove any very tough stems. Tear the leaves into bite-size pieces. There will be about 1½ pounds (4 to 6 cups packed).

2. In a large flameproof casserole, cook the garlic in the oil over moderately low heat, stirring occasionally, until the slices just begin to turn golden, 2 to 3 minutes. Immediately pour in the stock and add the dried pepper.

3. Raise the heat to moderately high and add the greens gradually, stirring them in until they are wilted. Cover the pot, reduce the heat to moderately low, and cook, stirring occasionally, until the greens are tender, about 45 minutes.

4. Stir in the beans. Add the lemon juice and vinegar and season with salt and pepper to taste.

➤ This dish is best freshly prepared. It can be reheated after up to 2 days in the refrigerator. I do not recommend freezing it.

Greek Green Bean Stew with Squash and Potatoes

4 to 6 Servings

I *am indebted for this exceptional recipe to Andrea Gilbert, whose work as a bilingual art editor has kept her in Athens for the past six years. Like many of the tastiest vegetable dishes, it is best made in summer, when you can obtain flat Romano beans (though we know them as Italian green beans, they are used in Greece for this kind of dish), and fresh squash, tomatoes, and pepper. As with most simple dishes, the freshness of the beans and the quality of the olive oil are important to the recipe's success.*

This stew is best eaten with crusty peasant bread, a slab of feta cheese, and a glass of hearty red wine. In Greece it is served at room temperature, though it is also good warm or cold.

> 2 pounds fresh flat Italian (Romano) green beans
> ½ cup fruity extra-virgin olive oil
> 1 medium-large onion, coarsely chopped
> 2 garlic cloves, chopped
> 2 large plum tomatoes (½ pound), peeled, seeded, and pureed in
>   a blender, or ¾ cup tomato puree
> 1½ teaspoons tomato paste
> 1 green bell pepper, cut lengthwise into ½-inch strips
> ¼ cup chopped flat Italian parsley
> 3 small red or gold potatoes (1 pound), peeled and cut into
>   6 to 8 wedges each
> 2 small zucchini (½ pound), cut into 1-inch rounds
> 2 small yellow summer squash (½ pound), cut into 1-inch rounds
> 1 teaspoon salt
> ½ teaspoon freshly ground black pepper

1. Trim the ends off the beans and pull off the strings. Cut into 2-inch lengths or leave whole. Cut the thick beans in half crosswise on the diagonal to expose the beans inside.

2. In a large flameproof casserole, heat the olive oil over moderate heat.

Add the onion and garlic and cook, stirring once or twice, until softened but not browned, 3 to 5 minutes.

3. Add the beans (pods and any loose inner beans), tomatoes, tomato paste, bell pepper, 2 tablespoons parsley, and ½ cup water. Stir to mix. Cover and simmer over moderately low heat, stirring occasionally, for 20 minutes, or until the beans are fairly soft.

4. Add the potatoes, zucchini, and summer squash to the beans, season with the salt and pepper and cook, covered, until all the vegetables are tender, 20 to 25 minutes. If the stew is too watery at this point, remove the vegetables with a slotted spoon and boil the liquid to thicken; then return the vegetables to the sauce. Remove from the heat and let stand until at least tepid. Season with additional salt and pepper to taste. Sprinkle the remaining parsley on top before serving.

➤ This dish keeps well for up to 2 days in the refrigerator. Let stand for about an hour, until it returns to room temperature, or warm over moderately low heat, stirring occasionally, or in a microwave oven. I do not recommend freezing this stew.

Grilled Vegetable Ragout with Goat Cheese Garlic Toasts

6 Servings

This is a delightful light stew, which serves well as either a starter or as a main course. While the grilling of the vegetables does take a little time and attention, it can be done in advance, and the last-minute assembly is simple and quick.

2 medium-small artichokes

1½ tablespoons lemon juice

6 Japanese eggplant, cut lengthwise in half

1 red bell pepper, halved and seeded

6 scallions, trimmed

3 small pattypan squash, split horizontally in half, or 6 baby pattypans

2 baby zucchini, sliced on an angle into large ovals about ½ inch thick

18 medium shiitake mushrooms (about ½ pound), stemmed

3½ tablespoons olive oil

3 shallots, minced

⅔ cup dry white wine

3½ cups Vegetable Stock (page 235) or Rich Chicken Stock (page 232)

1 teaspoon fresh lemon thyme leaves or ½ teaspoon dried leaves

Salt

Freshly ground black pepper

2 tablespoons minced fresh chives

Goat Cheese Garlic Toasts (recipe follows)

1. Cut off all but about 1 inch of the stems and the top third of both artichokes. Bend back and pull off the tough outer leaves. Clip off any remaining sharp tips. Cut each artichoke lengthwise into 4 thick slices; cut out the hairy chokes in the center. Rub the artichokes with lemon juice. Cook in a large saucepan of boiling salted water for 10 minutes; drain well and pat dry.

2. Prepare a moderately hot fire in a charcoal or gas grill. Brush the artichoke slices, eggplant, pepper, scallions, pattypan squash, zucchini slices, and shiitake mushroom caps with about 1½ tablespoons of the oil. Grill in batches if necessary, turning, until the vegetables are lightly browned. Cooking times will vary greatly, depending upon the vegetable: from 3 to 5 minutes for the zucchini and scallions to up to 10 minutes for the pattypan squash and pepper, so watch carefully. Try rotating the vegetables halfway before turning to produce those attractive crosshatch marks. As they are browned, remove the vegetables to a platter. Cut each pepper half into ½-inch-wide strips. The vegetables can be grilled several hours ahead and set aside at room temperature.

3. In a large, wide saucepan or flameproof casserole, heat the remaining 2 tablespoons olive oil over moderate heat. Add the shallots and cook until soft and fragrant, 1 to 2 minutes. Add the wine and boil until reduced by half, about 2 to 3 minutes. Add the stock and lemon thyme and simmer 5 minutes.

4. Add all the grilled vegetables to the stock, along with any juices that have collected on the platter. Simmer 2 minutes. Season with salt and pepper to taste. With a slotted spoon distribute the vegetables evenly among 6 soup plates. Ladle the broth over all and garnish with the minced chives. Serve at once, with the goat cheese garlic toasts on the side.

➤ All the elements of this dish can be prepared up to 4 hours in advance and set aside at room temperature. The finished dish is best eaten as soon as it is made. Leftovers can be reheated gently the next day. I do not recommend freezing this stew.

Vegetable and Bean Stews

Goat Cheese Garlic Toasts

Makes 12

>*6 large slices of French sourdough or peasant bread, cut about*
>   *½ inch thick*
>*2 or 3 garlic cloves, cut in half*
>*1 tablespoon extra-virgin olive oil*
>*3½ ounces fresh white goat cheese*
>*Herbes de Provence (optional)*

Toast the bread in a toaster or under the broiler until it is lightly browned.
Rub 1 side of each toast with a cut side of the garlic. Brush with the olive oil
and spread the goat cheese over the bread. If you like, dust with a light sprinkling
of herbes de Provence.

Dr. Fran's Italian Vegetable Stew

4 Servings

*F*ran Costa is a research psychologist at *the University of Colorado in Boulder. Her lean vegetarian version of her Italian grandmother's fennel sausage stew comes to me via a mutual friend. Eat it in a bowl with a slab of crusty bread or serve it over a thick pasta.*

> *3 tablespoons olive oil*
> *3 medium carrots, peeled and cut into 1½-inch chunks*
> *2 medium potatoes, peeled and cut into wedges*
> *1 medium onion, peeled and cut into wedges*
> *1 red bell pepper, cut into 1-inch squares*
> *1 medium zucchini, cut into 1-inch chunks*
> *5 ounces mushrooms, halved or quartered*
> *¾ teaspoon fennel seeds, lightly crushed*
> *1 (15-ounce) can stewed or Italian peeled tomatoes, with their juices*
> *1 (15-ounce) can chick-peas (garbanzo beans) drained*
> *1 bay leaf*
> *Salt*
> *Freshly ground black pepper*
> *¼ cup chopped fresh basil or 1 teaspoon dried*
> *Grated Romano cheese (optional but desirable)*

1. In a large pot, heat the olive oil over moderate heat. Cook the vegetables, stirring occasionally, as follows: Add the carrots and sauté 2 minutes. Add the potatoes and sauté 2 minutes. Add the onion and sauté 3 minutes. Add the bell pepper, zucchini, and mushrooms and sauté 3 minutes longer.

2. Stir in the fennel (and the dried basil). Add the tomatoes, their liquid, the chick-peas, and bay leaf. Bring to a boil, reduce the heat to low, and simmer, partially covered, until the vegetables are tender, 12 to 15 minutes.

3. Season with salt and pepper to taste. Remove and discard the bay leaf. Stir in the basil. Serve with a bowl of grated Romano cheese on the side.

➤ This dish is best eaten within several hours of being made. It can be reheated gently the next day. I do not recommend freezing it.

Navarin of Spring Vegetables

5 Servings

Light and elegant, this subtle mélange of spring vegetables in clear broth makes a marvelous first course. To extend it into a light lunch, accompany the stew with Goat Cheese Garlic Toasts (see page 220).

5 small spring artichokes

1 whole lemon plus 1½ tablespoons fresh lemon juice

¾ cup dry white wine

2 garlic cloves, smashed

½ teaspoon dried thyme leaves

1½ teaspoons salt

5 slim leeks

15 tiny red "creamer" potatoes (1 pound)

15 small white pearl onions (about 12 ounces), peeled

10 baby turnips or 3 small turnips, quartered

15 asparagus spears (about 1 pound)

4 tablespoons unsalted butter

3 shallots, minced

4 cups Rich Chicken Stock (page 232) or Vegetable Stock
   (page 235)

¼ teaspoon freshly ground pepper

1 tablespoon minced chives

1 tablespoon minced fresh chervil or 1½ teaspoons
   dried tarragon

1. Cut the stems and the top thirds off the artichokes. Bend back and pull off the tough outer leaves and trim off any remaining thorns. Cut the artichokes lengthwise in quarters and scoop out the hairy chokes. Cut the whole lemon in half, and as you work, rub the cut artichokes with the lemon to prevent discoloration.

2. In a large saucepan, combine the wine with ¾ cup water, the garlic, thyme, and 1 teaspoon of the salt. Bring to a boil. Squeeze any juice left from

the cut lemon into the water. Add the artichokes, cover, and steam, stirring them up occasionally for even cooking, until the artichoke pieces are tender, 10 to 12 minutes.

3. Meanwhile, trim the roots and the very tops from the leeks, but leave as much tender green as possible. Rinse them well to remove any grit, but do not cut lengthwise. Leave whole. Scrub the potatoes and peel off a band around their middles. Peel the pearl onions (see *Note*, page 15). Peel the turnips. Cut the tough stems off the bottoms of the asparagus and with a swivel-bladed vegetable peeler, peel off 2 to 3 inches of the thicker skin near the bottom of the spears.

4. Cook the potatoes in a large saucepan of boiling salted water until tender, 15 to 18 minutes. Drain into a colander. Cook the asparagus in a large skillet of boiling salted water until just barely tender, 2 to 3 minutes. Drain and rinse under cold running water; drain well.

5. In a large flameproof casserole, melt the butter. Add the shallots and cook over moderate heat until softened, 1 to 2 minutes. Add the stock and bring to a simmer. Add the pearl onions, cover, and simmer 5 minutes. Add the leeks and turnips, return to a boil, cover, and reduce the heat to moderately low. Simmer 10 to 15 minutes longer, or until the vegetables are just tender.

6. Season with the pepper and the remaining ½ teaspoon salt. Stir in the lemon juice. Add the artichokes, potatoes, and asparagus to the ragout and reheat for a minute or two. Ladle at once into soup plates, dividing the vegetables evenly. Garnish with the chives and chervil.

➤ Elements of this stew can be prepared through Step 4 up to several hours in advance and set aside at room temperature, but once finished, the dish is best eaten freshly cooked. Leftovers can be reheated gently the next day, but I do not recommend freezing this stew.

Rosemary Lentil Stew
with Goat Cheese and Sun-Dried
Tomatoes

6 to 8 Servings

Lentils have a particularly "meaty" flavor and texture, which makes them pleasing to nouveau vegetarians and to meat-eaters who choose to eat vegetarian several times a week. Since they don't need the long soaking of beans and cook in about half an hour, they give you much of the same nutrition with much less work time. If you simmer off the liquid, this stew can be served at room temperature as a distinctive salad or buffet side dish.

1 pound lentils

2 tablespoons olive oil

2 medium onions, chopped

2 celery ribs with leaves, finely diced

3 garlic cloves, minced

2 carrots, peeled and finely diced

1 (14½-ounce) can recipe-ready diced tomatoes, with their juices

6 cups Vegetable Stock (page 235), Rich Chicken Stock (page 232), or water

1½ teaspoons fresh rosemary, minced, or 1 teaspoon dried, crumbled, plus a few whole sprigs of fresh rosemary or parsley for garnish

1 bay leaf

⅛ teaspoon cayenne

1 or 2 smoked ham hocks (optional)

8 sun-dried tomato halves, cut into ¼-inch dice or ⅓ cup dried tomato bits

1 tablespoon extra-virgin olive oil

4 ounces fresh white goat cheese, cut into bits

Salt

Freshly ground black pepper

1. Rinse the lentils in a colander and pick over to remove any grit. Set aside.

2. In a large saucepan or flameproof casserole, heat the olive oil over moderate heat. Add the onions, cover, and cook 2 minutes. Uncover and cook, stirring occasionally, until they are golden and beginning to brown around the edges, 5 to 7 minutes. Add the celery and garlic and cook until the celery begins to soften, about 3 minutes longer.

3. Stir in the carrots and lentils. Add the tomatoes with their juices, the stock, rosemary, bay leaf, cayenne, and ham hock, if you are using it. Bring to a boil, skimming the foam off the top of the stew. Reduce the heat to moderately low and simmer, partially covered, 20 minutes.

4. Add the dried tomatoes and simmer 10 to 15 minutes longer, or until the lentils are tender but not mushy. Remove and discard the bay leaf. Remove the ham hock and discard, or reserve the meat for another use. Stir in the extra-virgin olive oil and goat cheese (it should remain in little clumps). Season with salt and pepper to taste. Serve at once or set aside at room temperature for up to 2 hours.

➤ This stew is best eaten shortly after it is finished, but it can be reheated after up to 2 days in the refrigerator. If you do so, you may have to add a bit more liquid, because the lentils will continue to absorb it. If it has thickened, the dish is good at room temperature as a salad. I do not recommend freezing this stew.

Vegetable Stew
with Spicy Peanut Sauce

6 Servings
Indonesian in flavor if not in origin, this hearty vegetable stew needs only a bowl of white or brown rice. It could also be served as a serious vegetable side dish with roast or grilled chicken, beef or lamb.

2½ tablespoons olive or other vegetable oil

1 large white onion, cut into 1-inch squares

2 medium carrots, peeled and cut on the diagonal into thin slices

1 red bell pepper, cut into 1-inch squares

1 yellow bell pepper, cut into 1-inch squares

1 tablespoon minced fresh ginger

4 garlic cloves—3 chopped, 1 crushed through a press

½ to 1 teaspoon crushed hot red pepper

1 pound cabbage, cut roughly into 1-inch pieces (see Note)

2 cups broccoli florets

2 cups cauliflower florets

1¾ cups Vegetable Stock (page 235), Rich Chicken Stock
     (page 232), or 1 (14½-ounce) can reduced-sodium broth

½ pound green beans, cut into 1½-inch pieces

½ cup peanut butter, preferably fresh

3 tablespoons Ketjap Manis (page 79) or 2 tablespoons soy sauce
     mixed with 2 tablespoons dark brown sugar

1½ tablespoons lemon juice

1 teaspoon sugar

¼ cup chopped dry-roasted peanuts

¼ cup chopped scallions

1. In a wok or large flameproof casserole, heat the oil over high heat. Add the onion and stir-fry until slightly softened and lightly browned around the edges, 2 to 3 minutes. Add the carrots, red and yellow peppers, ginger, chopped garlic, and hot pepper and stir-fry 2 minutes.

2. Add the cabbage and stir-fry until slightly wilted, 3 to 5 minutes. Add the broccoli, cauliflower, and 1½ cups of the stock. Bring to a boil, cover, reduce the heat to moderate and cook, stirring occasionally, 5 to 7 minutes, until the vegetables are just tender. Stir in the green beans.

3. Meanwhile, in a small bowl, stir the peanut butter with the remaining ¼ cup stock, the ketjap manis, lemon juice, sugar, and crushed garlic.

4. Stir the peanut sauce into the stew and simmer, uncovered, stirring occasionally, 5 minutes. Serve with the chopped peanuts and scallions sprinkled on top.

◇ **Note:** To cut up the cabbage easily, split in half lengthwise and cut out the tough core from each side. Cut each half into 1- to 1½-inch wedges and then cut crosswise into 1-inch pieces. Obviously, the outer pieces will be a little larger than the inner pieces. Exact size is not important.

➤ This dish is best served within several hours of preparation, but it can be reheated gently the next day. I do not recommend freezing it.

Stocks for Stews

This is a brief chapter because it is my belief that the simpler the stock, the more likely you are to make it, and only a few stocks are needed to prepare the recipes in this book. Homemade stocks are always the first choice for a first-class stew. While reduced-sodium canned chicken broth or vegetable broth can be used in a pinch, the results will not be as fine. But sometimes a little convenience is worth the savings in time; so wherever possible, I have listed it as an alternative. Where only a small amount of broth is called for, and the flavor won't be noticed under all the other seasonings, I have listed canned broth alone.

For chicken, there are two choices: Rich Chicken Stock, a clear, full-tasting broth made with a lot of chicken meat for flavor as well as bones for body, serves as the base for most of the chicken stews, a few of the veal and lamb stews, and for some of the vegetable stews. Where a darker color and more intense flavor are called for, Brown Chicken Stock is the preferred brew. In both cases, the recipes here make more than you'll need for one recipe; ladle the remainder into containers and freeze for future use. Anytime you poach chicken,

always strain and save the broth. However mild its taste, it will be better than water and probably better than canned chicken broth.

Most of the beef, veal, and venison stews, as well as some of the lamb and pork stews, call for Simple Meat Stock. Of course, a more elaborate brown stock that has simmered for days may yield a better-tasting stew. But I found that this easy recipe yielded excellent results, far better than any canned broth. Don't forget, in the stew the broth gets to simmer again, with all those big chunks of meat and vegetables, herbs, and spices; the sauce becomes more complex with the dish.

Since I hate the smell of fish stock simmering on my stove, and since good fresh fish bones are so hard to come by, all the seafood stews were developed to work with clam juice, which comes bottled or canned, or with water, white wine, or light chicken broth. Tomatoes and their juices also form the base of several of them.

Vegetable stews can almost always be made with chicken stock, though some do better with a pure vegetable flavor. For vegetarians, especially, a very good Vegetable Stock is included here as well. In a pinch, canned vegetable or chicken broth will work. I never use bouillon cubes. In all cases, stocks should be simmered salt-free, so that seasonings can be adjusted at the end.

Rich Chicken Stock

Makes 6 quarts

> *7 pounds chicken backs, necks, wings, gizzards, etc.*
> *(but no livers)*
> *1 whole chicken breast on the bone*
> *4 medium onions, cut in half*
> *2 whole cloves*
> *4 medium carrots, peeled and quartered*
> *3 celery ribs with leaves, quartered*
> *3 garlic cloves, smashed*
> *10 parsley stems*
> *1 bay leaf*
> *2 teaspoons black peppercorns*
> *½ cup mushroom trimmings and green leeks tops (optional)*

1. Rinse all the chicken well under cold running water. Place in a very large (preferably 16-quart) stockpot and add cold water to cover by 2 inches. Bring to a boil over moderate heat, frequently skimming the foam as it rises to the top.

2. Add all the remaining ingredients and enough additional cold water to reach 1 inch from the top of the pot. Reduce the heat to moderately low and simmer 3 to 5 hours, skimming occasionally. Add water as necessary to keep everything covered.

3. Strain the stock through a fine mesh sieve into a large bowl. If you have time, let cool and refrigerate overnight; then lift off the congealed fat and discard. If not, skim the fat from the top.

4. Return the stock to a large pot and boil until reduced to 6 quarts. If not using within 2 days, freeze up to 6 months in tightly covered containers.

Brown Chicken Stock

Makes 3 to 3½ quarts

2 tablespoons duck or goose fat or olive oil

2½ pounds chicken backs, necks, wings, gizzards (but no livers)

½- to ¾-pound chicken leg, thigh, and/or breast with the bones in

3 medium onions, halved

¾ cup mushroom stems and trimmings

2 medium carrots, thickly sliced

3 garlic cloves, smashed

8 sprigs of parsley

1 imported bay leaf

1 teaspoon black peppercorns

Pinch of dried thyme leaves

1. In a large flameproof casserole, heat the fat over moderately high heat. Add the chicken, onions, and mushrooms and cook, stirring occasionally, until nicely browned, about 20 minutes.

2. Add 2 cups of water and bring to a boil, scraping up the brown bits from the bottom of the pan. Add the carrots and garlic and enough water to cover by at least 1 inch. Bring to a boil, skimming off the foam as it rises to the top.

3. Add all the remaining ingredients, reduce the heat to moderately low, and simmer 3 to 4 hours, adding more water as necessary to keep the liquid at about the same level.

4. Strain through a fine mesh sieve and either skim all the fat off the top, or let cool, refrigerate overnight, and lift off and discard the congealed fat. Return to a clean pot and boil until reduced to 3 to 3½ quarts of rich-tasting stock. Freeze for up to 6 months.

Stocks for Stews

Simple Meat Stock

Makes 3½ to 4 quarts I make this stock as simple as possible so it can be seasoned to suit almost any soup. You can, if you wish, embellish it with a few garlic cloves, a carrot or two, a chopped tomato, or some mushroom stems, but it works beautifully with just the four ingredients listed below.

3 to 3½ pounds beef shank, center-cut
3 medium onions, quartered
2 imported bay leaves
½ teaspoon dried thyme leaves

1. Preheat the oven to 425 degrees F.

2. Place the beef shank and onions in a shallow roasting pan and roast, turning once, 45 to 55 minutes, or until the meat and onions are nicely browned. Transfer to a large stockpot.

3. Pour off any fat from the roasting pan. Pour 2 cups of water into the pan, set over moderately high heat, and bring to a boil, scraping up all the brown bits from the bottom of the pan. Pour into the stockpot.

4. Add 4½ to 5 more quarts of water to the stockpot and bring to a boil, skimming off any foam that rises to the top. Add the bay leaves and thyme, reduce the heat to moderately low and simmer, partially covered, 3½ to 4 hours.

5. Strain the stock. If there is more than 3½ to 4 quarts, boil to reduce. Skim the fat off the top. If you have time, it's easier to let it cool, then cover and refrigerate overnight; the next day, scrape the congealed fat off the top.

➤ Stored in a tightly closed container, this stock will keep well for up to 3 days in the refrigerator or up to 6 months in the freezer. To make usage simple, I divide it into 2- and 4-cup containers, so I can defrost just what I need for 1 dish.

Vegetable Stock

Makes 6 quarts

> *2 pounds onions, halved*
> *1 tablespoon olive oil*
> *1 pound carrots, peeled and thickly sliced*
> *1 pound potatoes, peeled and cut into chunks*
> *½ pound turnips, peeled and quartered*
> *½ pound mushrooms*
> *2 celery ribs with leaves*
> *4 garlic cloves*
> *2 imported bay leaves*
> *1 sprig of fresh thyme or ½ teaspoon dried leaves*
> *2 whole cloves*
> *1 teaspoon black peppercorns, coarsely cracked*
> *1 leek (white and all the green), split lengthwise and well rinsed,*
>   *then halved crosswise*
> *1 parsnip, peeled and quartered*
> *1 bunch of scallion greens (tops from about 6 scallions)*
> *4 large sprigs of Italian flat parsley*

1. Preheat the oven to 375 degrees F.

2. In a shallow roasting pan, toss the onions with the oil to coat. Bake, stirring once or twice, 45 minutes, or until nicely browned.

3. Transfer the onions to a stockpot. Pour 2 cups of water into the roasting pan and bring to a boil on top of the stove, scraping up any browned bits from the bottom of the pan. Pour the water into the stockpot.

4. Add all the remaining ingredients and 8 quarts of cold water. Bring to a boil, reduce the heat and simmer, partially covered, 2 hours. Strain and measure the liquid. If there is more than 6 quarts, boil to reduce. Let cool, then ladle into tightly covered containers and refrigerate for up to 3 days or freeze for up to 3 months.

Index